Summer Suppers

Good Housekeeping
Summer Suppers

COLLINS & BROWN

NOTES

- Both metric and imperial measures are given for the recipes. Follow either set of measures, not a mixture of both, as they are not interchangeable.
- All spoon measures are level.
  1 tsp = 5ml spoon; 1 tbsp = 15ml spoon.
- Ovens and grills must be preheated to the specified temperature.
- Use sea salt and freshly ground black pepper unless otherwise suggested.
- Fresh herbs should be used unless dried herbs are specified in a recipe.
- Medium eggs should be used except where otherwise specified. Free-range eggs are recommended.
- Note that certain recipes, including mayonnaise, lemon curd and some cold desserts, contain raw or lightly cooked eggs. The young, elderly, pregnant women and anyone with an immune-deficiency disease should avoid these, because of the slight risk of salmonella.
- Calorie counts per serving are provided for the recipes.

Contents

Foreword

I love the changing of the seasons and nothing excites me more than the time when spring turns slowly into summer. The days get warmer and become more carefree and lazy. There's a wealth of gorgeous produce in the shops, too. Soft English fruits, such as raspberries and strawberries, are everywhere and stone fruits, such as apricots and peaches, are at their best. Young veg, including courgettes and tomatoes, need very little doing to them so can be sliced and tossed in a dressing and served with a simple piece of marinated fish or meat for the perfect al fresco supper. This book of Summer Suppers provides something for every occasion.

Getting supper on the table has never been easier or simpler. Whether you fancy something light and quick, such as my favourite grilled ciabatta and mozzarella salad, or warming for the chilly nights as the summer draws to a close, like the roasted cod with fennel, you'll find it all here. And if you fancy something sweet, take your pick from the desserts chapter. Fruit kebabs with spiced pear dip, anyone? All the recipes have been triple tested in the Good Housekeeping Institute and so, when you come to make them, they'll look and taste just as delicious, too.

Emma

Emma Marsden

Cookery Editor

Good Housekeeping

Salads, Soups and Vegetarian Dishes

Freezing Tip

Cool, then freeze the soup in a sealed container at step 2 for up to three months.
To use, defrost in the fridge overnight. Reheat gently and simmer over a low heat for 5 minutes.

Beetroot Soup

1 tbsp olive oil

1 onion, finely chopped

750g (1lb 10oz) raw beetroot, peeled and cut into 1cm (½in) cubes

275g (10oz) potatoes, roughly chopped

2 litres (3½ pints) hot vegetable stock

juice of 1 lemon

8 tbsp soured cream

50g (2oz) mixed root vegetable crisps

salt and ground black pepper

3 tbsp chopped chives to garnish

1 Heat the olive oil in a large pan, add the onion and cook for 5 minutes. Add the vegetables and cook for a further 5 minutes.

2 Add the stock and lemon juice, then bring to the boil. Season with salt and pepper, reduce the heat and simmer, half-covered, for 25 minutes. Cool slightly, then whiz in a blender until smooth.

3 Pour the soup into a clean pan and reheat gently. Divide the soup among eight warmed bowls. Add 1 tbsp soured cream to each bowl, top with a few vegetable crisps and sprinkle the chopped chives on top to serve.`

Preparation Time: 15 minutes

Cooking Time: 40–45 minutes

Serves: 8

Calories Per Serving: 216

3 tbsp olive oil

2 tbsp lemon juice

150g (5oz) cooked pasta shapes, cooled

75g (3oz) feta cheese, crumbled

3 tomatoes, roughly chopped

2 tbsp small pitted black olives

½ cucumber, roughly chopped

1 small red onion, finely sliced

salt and ground black pepper

freshly chopped mint and lemon zest to garnish

Greek Pasta Salad

1 Mix the olive oil and lemon juice together in a salad bowl, then add the pasta, feta cheese, tomatoes, olives, cucumber and onion.

2 Season with salt and pepper, stir to mix, garnish with chopped mint and lemon zest and serve.

Preparation Time: 10 minutes

Cooking Time: 20 minutes

Serves: 2

Calories Per Serving: 382

1 large courgette, cut into chunks

1 red pepper, seeded and cut into chunks

12 cherry tomatoes

125g (4oz) halloumi cheese, cubed

100g (3½oz) natural yogurt

1 tsp ground cumin

2 tbsp olive oil

squeeze of lemon

1 lemon, cut into eight wedges

couscous tossed with freshly chopped flat-leafed parsley
to serve

Mediterranean Kebabs

1 Preheat the barbecue or grill. Soak eight wooden skewers in water for 20 minutes. Put the courgette into a large bowl with the red pepper, cherry tomatoes and halloumi cheese. Add the yogurt, cumin, olive oil and a squeeze of lemon and mix.

2 Push a lemon wedge on to each skewer, then divide the vegetables and cheese among the skewers. Grill the kebabs, turning regularly, for 8–10 minutes until the vegetables are tender and the halloumi is nicely charred. Serve with couscous.

Preparation Time: 15 minutes

Cooking Time: 8–10 minutes

Serves: 4

Calories Per Serving: 164

Red Onions with Rosemary Dressing

3 large red onions, root intact, each cut into eight wedges

6 tbsp olive oil

4 tbsp balsamic vinegar

2 tsp freshly chopped rosemary

salt and ground black pepper

1 Preheat the barbecue. Soak eight wooden skewers in water for 20 minutes. Thread the onion wedges on to the skewers. Brush with about 3 tbsp olive oil, then season well with salt and pepper.

2 Barbecue the onion kebabs for 30–35 minutes, turning from time to time and brushing with oil when necessary, until tender and lightly charred.

3 To make the dressing, mix together the balsamic vinegar, remaining olive oil and the rosemary. Drizzle the rosemary dressing over the cooked onions and serve.

Preparation Time: 20 minutes

Cooking Time: 30–35 minutes

Serves: 8

Calories Per Serving: 91

Warm Tofu, Fennel and Bean Salad

1 tbsp olive oil, plus 1 tsp

1 red onion, finely sliced

1 fennel bulb, finely sliced

1 tbsp cider vinegar

400g can butter beans, drained and rinsed

2 tbsp freshly chopped flat-leafed parsley

200g (7oz) smoked tofu, sliced into eight lengthways

salt and ground black pepper

1 Heat 1 tbsp olive oil in a large frying pan. Add the onion and fennel, and cook over a medium heat for 5–10 minutes. Add the cider vinegar and heat through for 2 minutes, then stir in the butter beans and parsley. Season with salt and pepper, then tip into a bowl.

2 Add the tofu to the pan with the remaining olive oil. Cook for 2 minutes on each side or until golden. Divide the bean mixture among four plates, add two slices of tofu to each plate and serve.

Preparation Time: 10 minutes

Cooking Time: 15 minutes

Serves: 4

Calories Per Serving: 150

Cook's Tip

Look out for marinated artichokes in supermarkets and delis; alternatively, buy canned artichoke hearts, drain, slice and cover in olive oil. They will keep in the refrigerator for up to one week.

8 thick slices Italian bread, such as ciabatta

2 tsp olive paste or sun-dried tomato paste

2 x 150g packs mozzarella cheese, drained and sliced

4 tbsp olive oil, plus extra for drizzling

2 tbsp balsamic vinegar

280g jar artichoke hearts in oil, drained and sliced (see Cook's Tip)

100g (3½oz) rocket salad

50g (2oz) sun-dried tomato halves

salt and ground black pepper

Grilled Ciabatta and Mozzarella Salad

1 Toast the bread slices on one side. Spread the untoasted side with olive or sun-dried tomato paste, then top with mozzarella slices and drizzle lightly with olive oil.

2 Mix the balsamic vinegar, salt and pepper in a bowl and whisk in the 4 tbsp olive oil. Add the artichoke hearts.

3 Place the bread slices under a preheated grill for 2–3 minutes or until the mozzarella browns lightly.

4 Toss the rocket salad with the artichoke mixture and divide between four plates. Top with two slices of grilled bread and the sun-dried tomatoes and serve.

Preparation Time: 10 minutes

Cooking Time: 5 minutes

Serves: 4

Calories Per Serving: 613

Cook's Tips

Peppadew peppers are from South Africa; sold in jars, they can be mild or hot.
Jalapeño chillies are from Mexico; they range from hot to fiery hot and when ripe they can be dark green or red; usually sold in jars.
Tahini is a paste made from finely ground sesame seeds. It is sold in jars.

Hummus with Rocket and Mint

3 tbsp sherry vinegar

75ml (3fl oz) extra virgin olive oil

150g (5oz) wild rocket leaves

12 small fresh mint leaves

12 Peppadew sweet piquant peppers (mild)

6 tbsp sliced jalapeño chillies (see Cook's Tips and page 17)

sesame seed flatbreads and lemon wedges to serve

For the hummus

400g can chickpeas, drained and rinsed

juice of 1 lemon

4 tbsp tahini (see Cook's Tips)

1 garlic clove, crushed

75ml (3fl oz) extra virgin olive oil

salt and ground black pepper

1 To make the hummus, put the chickpeas, lemon juice, tahini, garlic and olive oil in a food processor. Season well with salt and pepper, then whiz to a paste. Spoon the hummus into a non-metallic bowl, then cover and chill overnight.

2 To make the dressing, mix the sherry vinegar and a pinch of salt in a small bowl, then add the olive oil and whisk to combine. Chill overnight.

3 To serve, divide the hummus among six (150ml/¼ pint) pots. Put on to six plates. Put the rocket and mint leaves in a bowl, then drizzle the dressing over. Divide the salad, peppers, jalapeño chillies and flatbreads among the six plates. Serve with lemon wedges.

Preparation Time: 15 minutes, plus overnight chilling

Serves: 6

Calories Per Serving: 399

Cook's Tips

Red bird's eye chillies are always very hot. The smaller they are, the hotter they are. **Be extremely careful** when handling chillies not to touch or rub your eyes with your fingers, as they will sting. As a precaution, use rubber gloves when preparing them if you like. Wash knives immediately after handling chillies for the same reason.

Thai Noodle Salad

200g (7oz) sugarsnap peas, trimmed

250g pack Thai stir-fry rice noodles

100g (3½oz) cashew nuts

300g (11oz) carrots, cut into batons

10 spring onions, sliced on the diagonal

300g (11oz) bean sprouts

20g (¾oz) fresh coriander, roughly chopped, plus coriander sprigs to garnish

1 red bird's eye chilli, seeded and finely chopped (see Cook's Tips)

2 tsp sweet chilli sauce

4 tbsp sesame oil

6 tbsp soy sauce

juice of 2 limes

salt and ground black pepper

1 Bring a pan of salted water to the boil and blanch the sugarsnap peas for 2–3 minutes until just tender to the bite. Drain and refresh under cold water.

2 Put the noodles into a bowl, cover with boiling water and leave to soak for 4 minutes. Rinse under cold water and drain very well.

3 Toast the cashews in a dry frying pan until golden – about 5 minutes.

4 Put the sugarsnaps in a large glass serving bowl. Add the carrots, spring onions, bean sprouts, chopped coriander, chopped chilli, cashews and noodles. Mix together the chilli sauce, sesame oil, soy sauce and lime juice and season well with salt and pepper. Pour over the salad, toss together, garnish with coriander sprigs and serve.

Preparation Time: 20 minutes, plus 4 minutes soaking

Cooking Time: 7–8 minutes

Serves: 4

Calories Per Serving: 568

Spinach and Rice Soup

4 tbsp extra virgin olive oil

1 onion, finely chopped

2 garlic cloves, crushed

2 tsp freshly chopped thyme or a large pinch of dried thyme

2 tsp freshly chopped rosemary or a large pinch of dried rosemary

zest of ½ lemon

2 tsp ground coriander

¼ tsp cayenne pepper

125g (4oz) arborio (risotto) rice

1.1 litres (2 pints) vegetable stock

225g (8oz) fresh or frozen and thawed spinach, shredded

4 tbsp pesto sauce

salt and ground black pepper

extra virgin olive oil and freshly grated Parmesan to serve

1 Heat half the olive oil in a pan. Add the onion, garlic, herbs, lemon zest and spices, then fry gently for 5 minutes.

2 Add the remaining oil with the rice and cook, stirring, for 1 minute. Add the stock, bring to the boil and simmer gently for 20 minutes or until the rice is tender.

3 Stir the spinach into the soup with the pesto sauce. Cook for 2 minutes, then season to taste with salt and pepper.

4 Serve drizzled with a little olive oil and topped with Parmesan.

Preparation Time: 10 minutes

Cooking Time: 25–30 minutes

Serves: 4

Calories Per Serving: 336

Try Something Different

Use papaya instead of mango.
Ginger and chilli dressing: mix together 2 tsp grated fresh root ginger, 1 tbsp sweet chilli sauce, 2 tsp white wine vinegar and 2 tbsp walnut oil. Season with salt.
Peanut dressing: mix together 1 tbsp peanut butter, ¼ crushed dried chilli, 4 tsp white wine vinegar, 3 tbsp walnut oil, 1 tsp sesame oil and a dash of soy sauce.

Sprouted Bean and Mango Salad

3 tbsp mango chutney

grated zest and juice of 1 lime

2 tbsp olive oil

4 plum tomatoes

1 small red onion, finely chopped

1 red pepper, seeded and finely diced

1 yellow pepper, seeded and finely diced

1 mango, finely diced

4 tbsp freshly chopped coriander

150g (5oz) sprouted beans

salt and ground black pepper

1 To make the dressing, place the mango chutney in a small bowl and add the lime zest and juice. Whisk in the olive oil and season with salt and pepper.

2 Quarter the tomatoes, discard the seeds and then dice. Put into a large bowl with the onion, peppers, mango, coriander and sprouted beans. Pour the dressing over and mix well. Serve the salad immediately.

Preparation Time: 15 minutes

Serves: 6

Calories Per Serving: 103

Cook's Tip

Bulgur wheat is widely used in Middle Eastern cooking and has a light, nutty flavour and texture. It is available in several different sizes – from coarse to fine.

175g (6oz) bulgur wheat (see Cook's Tip)

700g (1½lb) cherry tomatoes or baby plum tomatoes

8 tbsp extra virgin olive oil

a handful each of fresh mint and basil, roughly chopped, plus fresh basil sprigs to garnish

3–4 tbsp balsamic vinegar

1 bunch spring onions, sliced

salt and ground black pepper

Roasted Tomato Bulgur Salad

1 Put the bulgur wheat in a bowl and add boiling water to cover by 1cm (½in). Leave to soak for 30 minutes.

2 Preheat the oven to 220°C (200°C fan oven) mark 7. Put the tomatoes in a small roasting tin, drizzle with half the olive oil and add half the mint. Season with salt and pepper, and roast for 10–15 minutes until beginning to soften.

3 Put the remaining oil and the balsamic vinegar into a large bowl. Add the warm pan juices from the roasted tomatoes and the soaked bulgur wheat.

4 Stir in the remaining chopped herbs and the spring onions, and check the seasoning. You may need a little more vinegar depending on the sweetness of the tomatoes.

5 Carefully toss in the tomatoes and serve garnished with basil sprigs.

Preparation Time: 10 minutes, plus 30 minutes soaking

Cooking Time: 10–15 minutes

Serves: 6

Calories Per Serving: 225

Polenta with Mixed Mushrooms

50g (2oz) butter

1.1kg (2½lb) mixed mushrooms

1 red chilli, seeded and finely chopped (see page 17)

3 garlic cloves, sliced

100g (3½oz) sun-dried tomatoes, roughly chopped

1 tsp chopped fresh thyme, plus thyme sprigs to garnish

1kg (2¼lb) ready-made polenta

3 tbsp olive oil

truffle oil (optional)

salt and ground black pepper

1 Melt half the butter in a deep-sided frying pan or wok. Add half the mushrooms and cook over a high heat until all the liquid has evaporated, then set aside. Repeat with the remaining butter and mushrooms. Add the chilli and garlic to the pan and fry for 2 minutes, then add to the mushrooms, together with the sun-dried tomatoes and chopped thyme. Mix well and season with salt and pepper.

2 Slice the polenta into 12 pieces, about 1cm (½in) thick. Heat the olive oil in a non-stick frying pan. Add the polenta in batches, and fry for 3–4 minutes on each side or until golden.

3 To serve, arrange two slices of polenta per person on a plate, top with the mushroom mixture and drizzle with a little truffle oil, if using. Garnish with thyme sprigs.

Preparation Time: 10 minutes

Cooking Time: 20 minutes

Serves: 6

Calories Per Serving: 383

Sweet Chilli Tofu Stir-fry

200g (7oz) firm tofu

4 tbsp sweet chilli sauce

2 tbsp light soy sauce

1 tbsp sesame seeds

2 tbsp toasted sesame oil

600g (1lb 5oz) ready-prepared mixed stir-fry vegetables, such as carrots, broccoli, mangetouts and bean sprouts

a handful of pea shoots or young salad leaves to garnish

1 Drain the tofu, pat it dry and cut it into large cubes. Put the tofu in a shallow container and pour over 1 tbsp sweet chilli sauce and 1 tbsp light soy sauce. Cover and marinate for 10 minutes.

2 Meanwhile, toast the sesame seeds in a hot wok or large frying pan until golden. Tip on to a plate.

3 Return the wok or frying pan to the heat and add 1 tbsp sesame oil. Add the marinated tofu and stir-fry for 5 minutes until golden. Remove and set aside.

4 Heat the remaining sesame oil in the pan, add the vegetables and stir-fry for 3–4 minutes until just tender. Stir in the cooked tofu.

5 Pour the remaining sweet chilli sauce and soy sauce into the pan, toss well and cook for a further 1 minute until heated through. Sprinkle with the toasted sesame seeds and pea shoots or salad leaves and serve immediately.

Preparation Time: 5 minutes, plus 10 minutes marinating

Cooking Time: 12 minutes

Serves: 4

Calories Per Serving: 167

125g (4oz) plain flour, plus 2 tbsp extra to sprinkle

2 tbsp cornflour

2 tbsp arrowroot

125g (4oz) cauliflower, cut into small florets

2 large carrots, cut into matchsticks

16 button mushrooms

2 courgettes, sliced

2 red peppers, seeded and sliced

vegetable oil for deep-frying

salt and ground black pepper

fresh coriander sprigs to garnish

For the dipping sauce

25g (1oz) fresh root ginger, peeled and grated

4 tbsp dry sherry

3 tbsp soy sauce

Vegetable Tempura

1 Sift 125g (4oz) flour, the cornflour and arrowroot into a large bowl with a pinch each of salt and pepper. Gradually whisk in 300ml (½ pint) ice-cold water to form a thin batter. Cover and chill.

2 To make the dipping sauce, put the ginger, sherry and soy sauce in a heatproof bowl and pour over 200ml (7fl oz) boiling water. Stir well to mix, then set aside.

3 Put the vegetables in a large bowl and sprinkle over 2 tbsp flour. Toss well to coat. Heat the oil in a wok or deep-fryer to 170°C (test by frying a small cube of bread; it should brown in 40 seconds).

4 Dip a handful of the vegetables in the batter, then remove with a slotted spoon, taking up a lot of the batter with the vegetables. Add to the hot oil and deep-fry for 3–5 minutes until crisp and golden. Remove with a slotted spoon and drain on kitchen paper; keep them hot while you cook the remaining batches. Serve immediately, garnished with coriander sprigs and accompanied by the dipping sauce.

Preparation Time: 20 minutes

Cooking Time: 15 minutes

Serves: 4

Calories Per Serving: 450

Health Tip

Raw garlic is a wonderful tonic for your health and is believed to have curative and protective powers, including lowering blood pressure and cholesterol levels.
Look out for fresh garlic during the summer months – it has a milder flavour.

Cucumber, Yogurt and Mint Soup

1 cucumber, coarsely grated

500g (1lb 2oz) Greek yogurt

a generous handful of fresh mint leaves, chopped

1 large garlic clove, crushed

125ml (4fl oz) cold water or light vegetable or chicken stock

salt and ground black pepper

6 ice cubes and fresh mint sprigs to serve

1 Set aside 6 tbsp of the cucumber. Put the remainder into a large bowl with all the remaining ingredients for the soup and mix together. Chill until required.

2 Before serving, stir the soup, then taste and adjust the seasoning. Spoon the soup into six bowls and drop an ice cube, 1 tbsp of the reserved cucumber and a few mint sprigs into each bowl.

Preparation Time: 15 minutes, plus chilling

Serves: 6

Calories Per Serving: 105

Try Something Different

Yogurt dressing: mix together 5 tbsp natural yogurt with 1 tbsp each freshly chopped mint and chives and a small crushed garlic clove. Season with salt and pepper.

Tomato dressing: halve and seed 8 cherry tomatoes and cut into thin strips. Mix 1 tbsp balsamic vinegar with 3 tbsp olive oil, 2 tbsp freshly chopped tarragon, salt and pepper. Stir in the tomato and drizzle over the vegetables.

Summer Vegetable Salad

600g (1lb 5oz) mixed green vegetables, such as green beans, peas, sugarsnap peas, trimmed asparagus, broad beans, broccoli

¼ small cucumber, halved, seeded and sliced

2 tbsp freshly chopped flat-leafed parsley

For the dressing

1 tbsp white wine vinegar or sherry vinegar

1 tsp English mustard powder

3 tbsp extra virgin olive oil

salt and ground black pepper

1 Cook the beans in a large pan of lightly salted boiling water for 3 minutes, then add all the other vegetables. Return the water to the boil and cook for a further 3–4 minutes. Drain well and put immediately into a bowl of ice-cold water.

2 Whisk all the dressing ingredients together and season with salt and pepper.

3 To serve, drain the vegetables and then toss in the dressing with the cucumber and parsley.

Preparation Time: 10 minutes

Cooking Time: 6–7 minutes

Serves: 4

Calories Per Serving: 119

Cook's Tips

To serve this dish hot, put 5 tbsp basil-infused oil in a frying pan, add the garlic and chillies and cook for 1 minute. Add the drained pasta and mix well, then add the tomatoes and mozzarella. Garnish and serve.
Instead of mozzarella, use Gorgonzola or Brie.
You can use ½ tsp dried crushed chillies instead of fresh.

Tomato and Mozzarella Pasta Salad

2 tsp lemon juice

7 tbsp basil-infused olive oil

2 garlic cloves, crushed

350g (12oz) penne pasta

250g (9oz) mozzarella, cut into chunks

700g (1½lb) vine-ripened tomatoes, skinned, seeded and cut into chunks

½ large red chilli, seeded and finely sliced (see page 17)

½ large green chilli, seeded and finely sliced (see page 17)

salt and ground black pepper

fresh flat-leafed parsley or basil to garnish

1 Put some salt and pepper in a small bowl, whisk in the lemon juice, followed by the flavoured oil and garlic, then set aside.

2 Bring a large pan of salted water to the boil, add the pasta and cook according to the packet instructions. Drain well, then tip into a large bowl and toss with 2 tbsp of the dressing (this will prevent the pasta from sticking together); set aside to cool. Put the mozzarella in a large bowl with the remaining dressing and set aside.

3 When ready to serve (see Cook's Tips), add the pasta to the mozzarella with the tomatoes and chillies. Toss together and season well with salt and pepper. Garnish with parsley or basil, then serve.

Preparation Time: 20 minutes, plus cooling

Cooking Time: 10–12 minutes

Serves: 4

Calories Per Serving: 665

Get Ahead

Complete the recipe up to the end of step 2, then leave the pears in the frying pan and set aside for up to 4 hours.
To use Warm the pears in the pan for 1 minute, then complete the recipe.

50g (2oz) walnut pieces

1 tbsp walnut or mild olive oil

small knob of butter

3 firm rosy pears, quartered, cored and thickly sliced

1 bag Caesar salad with croûtons, dressing and Parmesan

100g (3½oz) blue cheese, such as Roquefort, Stilton or Danish blue, crumbled

1 bunch chives, roughly chopped

Warm Pear and Walnut Caesar Salad

1 Dry-fry the walnuts in a non-stick frying pan over a medium heat for about 1 minute until lightly toasted. Set aside.

2 Heat the oil and butter in the pan, then add the pears. Fry for 2 minutes on each side or until golden. Remove with a slotted spoon.

3 To serve, put the salad leaves into a large bowl. Add the walnuts, pears, croûtons, Parmesan and blue cheese. Add the salad dressing and toss lightly, or serve the dressing separately in a small bowl. Serve immediately, garnished with chives.

Preparation Time: 10 minutes

Cooking Time: 5 minutes

Serves: 6

Calories Per Serving: 397

Grilled Mediterranean Vegetables

6 garlic cloves

2 red peppers, seeded and cut into thick strips

4 courgettes, quartered lengthways and cut into sticks

2 aubergines, cut into sticks the same size as the courgettes

2 small red onions, cut into wedges

100ml (3½fl oz) olive oil

salt and ground black pepper

1 Blanch the whole cloves of garlic in boiling water for 5 minutes.

2 Put all the vegetables into a shallow glass dish and pour the olive oil over. Season with salt and pepper. Cover and chill for up to 6 hours.

3 Preheat the barbecue, griddle or grill. Lay the vegetables in a single layer on the grill rack (you may need to do two batches) and cook for about 10 minutes, turning once or twice, until they are slightly charred. Serve hot or cold.

Preparation Time: 10 minutes, plus 6 hours chilling

Cooking Time: 20 minutes

Serves: 4

Calories Per Serving: 234

Cook's Tip

Banana leaves are sometimes used instead of plates in South-east Asia; they make an unusual presentation and are available from some Asian food shops.

Courgettes with Sesame Seeds

2 tbsp sesame seeds

2 tbsp vegetable oil

4 garlic cloves, crushed

900g (2lb) courgettes, thinly sliced

1 spring onion, thickly sliced

½ tsp salt

1 tbsp sesame oil

ground black pepper

banana leaves to serve (optional, see Cook's Tip)

1 Toast the sesame seeds in a hot wok or large frying pan until golden. Tip on to a plate.

2 Heat the vegetable oil in the wok or frying pan. Add the garlic and fry for 2 minutes.

3 Add the courgettes and stir-fry for 7–8 minutes. Stir in the spring onion, salt and sesame oil. Season to taste with pepper. Cook for a further 1 minute, then add the toasted sesame seeds. Stir once and serve hot or cold on a bed of banana leaves, if you like.

Preparation Time: 5 minutes

Cooking Time: 12 minutes

Serves: 6

Calories Per Serving: 107

Crispy Noodles with Hot Sweet and Sour Sauce

vegetable oil for deep-frying

125g (4oz) rice or egg noodles

frisée leaves to serve

For the sauce

2 tbsp vegetable oil

1 garlic clove, crushed

1cm (½in) piece fresh root ginger, peeled and grated

6 spring onions, sliced

½ red pepper, seeded and finely chopped

2 tbsp sugar

2 tbsp malt vinegar

2 tbsp tomato ketchup

2 tbsp dark soy sauce

2 tbsp dry sherry

1 tbsp cornflour

1 tbsp sliced green chillies (see page 17)

1 First, make the sauce. Heat the vegetable oil in a wok or large frying pan and stir-fry the garlic, ginger, spring onions and red pepper for 1 minute. Stir in the sugar, malt vinegar, ketchup, soy sauce and sherry. Blend the cornflour with 8 tbsp water and stir it into the sauce. Cook for 2 minutes, stirring. Add the chillies, cover and keep the sauce warm.

2 Heat the vegetable oil in a deep-fryer to 190°C (test by frying a small cube of bread; it should brown in 20 seconds). Cut the noodles into six portions and fry, a batch at a time, very briefly until lightly golden (take care as the hot oil rises up quickly).

3 Drain the noodles on kitchen paper and keep them warm while you cook the remainder.

4 Arrange the noodles on a bed of frisée leaves and serve immediately with the sauce served separately.

Preparation Time: 10 minutes

Cooking Time: about 15 minutes

Serves: 4

Calories Per Serving: 317

Try Something Different

Vary the vegetables, but always blanch the harder ones first. For a winter vegetable stir-fry, use cauliflower and broccoli florets, carrot sticks, 2–3 sliced spring onions and a little chopped fresh root ginger.

Summer Vegetable Stir-fry

1 Blanch the carrots in lightly salted boiling water for 2 minutes, then drain and pat dry.

2 Toast the sesame seeds in a hot dry wok or large frying pan over a medium heat, stirring until they turn golden. Tip on to a plate.

3 Return the wok or frying pan to the heat, add the sunflower oil and heat until it is smoking. Add the garlic to the oil and stir-fry for 20 seconds. Add the carrots, courgettes, yellow pepper and asparagus. Stir-fry over a high heat for 1 minute.

4 Add the cherry tomatoes and season to taste with salt and pepper. Stir-fry for 3–4 minutes until the vegetables are just tender. Add the vinegar and sesame oil, toss well and sprinkle with the toasted sesame seeds. Serve immediately.

125g (4oz) baby carrots, scrubbed and trimmed

1 tbsp sesame seeds

2 tbsp sunflower oil

2 garlic cloves, roughly chopped

125g (4oz) baby courgettes, halved lengthways

1 large yellow pepper, seeded and cut into thick strips

125g (4oz) thin asparagus spears, trimmed

125g (4oz) cherry tomatoes, halved

2 tbsp balsamic or sherry vinegar

1 tsp sesame oil

salt and ground black pepper

Preparation Time: 15 minutes

Cooking Time: 7–8 minutes

Serves: 4

Calories Per Serving: 78

Try Something Different

Cherry tomato and rocket frittata: replace the courgettes with 175g (6oz) ripe cherry tomatoes, frying them for 1 minute only, until they begin to soften. Immediately after pouring in the eggs, scatter 25g (1oz) rocket leaves over the surface. Continue cooking as in step 3.

Courgette and Parmesan Frittata

40g (1½oz) butter

1 small onion, finely chopped

225g (8oz) courgettes, trimmed and finely sliced

6 eggs, beaten

25g (1oz) Parmesan, freshly grated, plus shavings to garnish

salt and ground black pepper

green salad to serve

1 Melt 25g (1oz) butter in an 18cm (7in) non-stick frying pan and cook the onion for about 10 minutes until softened. Add the courgettes and fry gently for 5 minutes or until they begin to soften.

2 Beat the eggs in a bowl and season with salt and pepper.

3 Add the remaining butter to the pan and heat, then pour in the eggs. Cook for 2–3 minutes or until golden underneath and cooked around the edges. Meanwhile, preheat the grill to medium.

4 Sprinkle the grated cheese over the frittata and grill for 1–2 minutes until just set. Scatter with Parmesan shavings, cut into quarters and serve with a green salad.

Preparation Time: 10 minutes

Cooking Time: 15–20 minutes

Serves: 4

Calories Per Serving: 229

Try Something Different

Thinly sliced mushrooms, diced red pepper, cubes of tofu (not silken) or cooked broccoli or asparagus spears can all be added. Add to the salad just before serving, and mix well.

Japanese Noodle Salad

2 tbsp sesame seeds

200g (7oz) Japanese 100% wheat-free soba noodles

2–3 tbsp tamari (wheat-free Japanese soy sauce)

1 tbsp sesame oil

1 tbsp rice vinegar

salt

small bunch spring onions, finely sliced, to serve

1 Toast the sesame seeds in a dry frying pan until golden. Set aside.

2 Cook the noodles in a pan of lightly salted boiling water for 5 minutes or until tender but firm. Drain and cool under cold running water. Drain again and put into a bowl.

3 Add the toasted sesame seeds, tamari, sesame oil and rice vinegar and toss to coat the noodles. Chill until needed or for up to 24 hours. To serve, top with spring onions.

Preparation Time: 2 minutes, plus chilling

Cooking Time: 7 minutes

Serves: 4

Calories Per Serving: 268

Try Something Different

Add a handful of sultanas or raisins, or lightly toasted sesame seeds.

Spinach and Carrot Salad

350g (12oz) carrots, sliced

225g (8oz) green beans, trimmed

350g (12oz) baby leaf spinach

1 garlic clove, crushed

2 tsp each soy sauce and honey

1 tbsp cider vinegar

4 tbsp olive oil

ground black pepper

1 Cook the carrots in lightly salted boiling water for 3–4 minutes, adding the beans for the last minute. Drain and rinse in cold water. Drain well, then put both in a bowl with the spinach.

2 Put the crushed garlic in a small bowl. Add the soy sauce, honey, cider vinegar and olive oil. Season with pepper and whisk together thoroughly. Pour some of the dressing over the carrot, bean and spinach mixture and toss together well. Serve the remaining dressing separately.

Preparation Time: 5 minutes

Cooking Time: 4 minutes

Serves: 4

Calories Per Serving: 173 calories

Try Something Different

Instead of rosemary use a small handful of fresh coriander and add a dash or two of Tabasco before serving.

3 rosemary sprigs

400g (14oz) jar roasted red peppers, drained

2 tsp golden caster sugar

1 litre (1¾ pints) tomato juice

4 very ripe plum tomatoes

300ml (½ pint) hot chicken stock

450ml (¾ pint) freshly squeezed orange juice

ground black pepper

Tomato, Pepper and Orange Soup

1 Pull the leaves from the rosemary sprigs and discard the twiggy stalks. Put the leaves into a food processor or blender, add the peppers, caster sugar, half the tomato juice and the plum tomatoes and whiz together until slightly chunky.

2 Sieve the mixture into a pan and stir in the stock, orange juice and the remaining tomato juice. Bring to the boil and simmer gently for about 10 minutes. Season with plenty of pepper to serve.

Preparation Time: 15 minutes

Cooking Time: 12 minutes

Serves: 4

Calories Per Serving: 136

Cook's Tip

Halloumi is a firm cheese made from cow's, goat's, or sheep's milk. It has a mild, salty flavour and is best used sliced and cooked.

250g (9oz) halloumi, sliced into eight (see Cook's Tip)

1 tbsp flour, seasoned

2 tbsp olive oil

200g (7oz) mixed leaf salad

2 avocados, halved, stoned, peeled and sliced

fresh rocket leaves to garnish

lemon halves to serve

For the mint dressing

3 tbsp lemon juice

8 tbsp olive oil

3 tbsp freshly chopped mint

salt and ground black pepper

Halloumi and Avocado Salad

1 To make the dressing, whisk the lemon juice with the olive oil and mint, then season with salt and pepper.

2 Coat the halloumi with the flour. Heat the olive oil in a large frying pan and fry the cheese for 1 minute on each side or until it forms a golden crust.

3 Meanwhile, in a large bowl, add half the dressing to the salad leaves and avocado and toss together. Arrange the hot cheese on top and drizzle the remaining dressing over. Garnish with rocket leaves and serve with lemon halves to squeeze over.

Preparation Time: 10 minutes

Cooking Time: 2 minutes

Serves: 4

Calories Per Serving: 397

Cook's Tip

The root vegetables take longest to cook through, while the asparagus and leeks only need a short time under the grill.

Grilled Vegetables with Walnut Sauce

2 large carrots, peeled and cut into 5mm (¼in) slices

1 fennel bulb, thinly sliced lengthways

225g (8oz) sweet potatoes, peeled and thinly sliced

225g (8oz) Jerusalem artichokes, scrubbed and thinly sliced

225g (8oz) thick asparagus spears, trimmed

8 baby leeks, trimmed

4–6 tbsp olive oil

For the walnut sauce

50g (2oz) day-old bread, crusts removed

75g (3oz) walnuts, toasted

2 garlic cloves, chopped

1 tbsp red wine vinegar

2 tbsp chopped parsley

90ml (3fl oz) olive oil

50ml (2fl oz) walnut oil

salt and ground black pepper

1 First make the walnut sauce. Crumble the bread into a bowl, add 2 tbsp water, then squeeze dry. Put the bread into a food processor with the toasted walnuts, garlic, wine vinegar and parsley; blend until fairly smooth. Add the olive and walnut oils and process briefly to form a thick sauce. Season with salt and pepper and transfer to a serving dish.

2 Preheat the grill to medium-high. Baste the vegetables with olive oil and grill in batches, turning once, for 2–6 minutes on each side until charred and tender (see Cook's Tip); keep warm in a low oven while grilling the rest.

3 Transfer all the grilled vegetables to a warmed serving plate and season with a little salt and pepper. Serve accompanied by the walnut sauce.

Preparation Time: 25 minutes

Cooking Time: 15–20 minutes

Serves: 4

Calories Per Serving: 598

Cook's Tip

It's best to roast vegetables in a single layer or they will steam and become soggy. Use two tins if necessary.

Roasted Vegetable Salad with Mustard Mayonnaise

900g (2lb) mixed vegetables, such as fennel, courgettes, leeks, aubergines, baby turnips, new potatoes and red onions

2 garlic cloves, unpeeled

4–5 fresh marjoram or rosemary sprigs

5 tbsp olive oil

1 tsp flaked sea salt

mixed crushed peppercorns to taste

4 tsp balsamic vinegar

warm crusty bread to serve

For the mustard mayonnaise

150ml (¼ pint) mayonnaise

2 tbsp Dijon mustard

salt and ground black pepper

1 Preheat the oven to 220°C (200°C fan oven) mark 7. For the vegetables, quarter the fennel, chop the courgettes, leeks and aubergines, trim the turnips and cut the onions into petals. Place the vegetables, garlic, marjoram or rosemary, the olive oil, salt and peppercorns in a roasting tin and toss well (see Cook's Tip).

2 Cook in the oven for 30–35 minutes or until the vegetables are golden, tossing frequently. Sprinkle the balsamic vinegar over and return to the oven for a further 5 minutes.

3 To make the mustard mayonnaise, mix together the mayonnaise and mustard, then season with salt and pepper and set aside.

4 Arrange the vegetable salad on a serving dish and serve with the mustard mayonnaise and crusty bread.

Preparation Time: 15 minutes

Cooking Time: 40 minutes

Serves: 4

Calories Per Serving: 420

2 tbsp olive oil, plus extra to grease

300ml (½ pint) semi-skimmed milk

10 fresh sage leaves, roughly chopped

125g (4oz) quick-cook polenta

2 garlic cloves, crushed

25g (1oz) butter

100g (3½oz) salad leaves

125g (4oz) Gorgonzola cheese, cut into cubes

125g (4oz) each sunblush tomatoes and roasted red peppers

salt and ground black pepper

Griddled Polenta with Gorgonzola Salad

1 Lightly oil a 450g (1lb) loaf tin. Put the milk in a pan, then add the sage, 1 scant tsp salt and 300ml (½ pint) water and bring to the boil. Add the polenta to the pan in a thin, steady stream, stirring, to make a smooth paste.

2 Reduce the heat, add the garlic and cook for about 8 minutes, stirring occasionally. Add the olive oil, then season with pepper and stir well. Press into the prepared loaf tin, smooth the top and leave to cool for 45 minutes.

3 Once the polenta is cool, turn out on to a board and cut into eight slices.

4 Melt the butter in a griddle pan and fry the polenta slices on each side until golden.

5 Divide among four plates. Add the salad, Gorgonzola, sunblush tomatoes and red peppers, and serve.

Preparation Time: 20 minutes, plus 45 minutes cooling

Cooking Time: 20 minutes

Serves: 4

Calories Per Serving: 362

Poultry and Meat

4 tbsp hot mango chutney (or ordinary mango chutney, plus
½ tsp Tabasco)

grated zest and juice of 1 lime

4 tbsp natural yogurt

2 tbsp freshly chopped coriander

1 small green chilli (optional), seeded and finely chopped
(see page 17)

4 chicken breasts with skin on

1 large ripe mango

oil to brush

salt and ground black pepper

fresh coriander sprigs and lime wedges to garnish

Fiery Mango Chicken

1 Mix together the chutney, lime zest and juice, yogurt, chopped coriander and, if you like it spicy, the finely chopped chilli.

2 Put the chicken breasts, skin side down, on the worksurface, cover with clingfilm and lightly beat with a rolling pin. Slice each into three pieces and put into the yogurt mixture; stir to coat. Cover and chill for at least 30 minutes or overnight.

3 Preheat the barbecue or grill. Peel and stone the mango, then slice into four thick pieces. Brush lightly with oil and season well with salt and pepper. Barbecue or grill for about 2 minutes on each side; the fruit should be lightly charred but still firm. Put to one side.

4 Barbecue or grill the chicken for 3–5 minutes on each side until golden. Serve with the grilled mango, garnished with coriander and lime wedges.

Preparation Time: 15 minutes, plus minimum
30 minutes marinating

Cooking Time: 10 minutes

Serves: 4

Calories Per Serving: 220

Cook's Tip

Salt-baked new potatoes: toss 550g (1¼lb) par-boiled new potatoes with 2 tbsp olive oil and 1 tbsp sea salt flakes. Cook at 200°C (180°C fan oven) mark 6 for 40 minutes until tender.

Peppercorn Steaks with Aïoli

1 garlic clove, crushed

1 tbsp olive oil

2 tbsp mixed peppercorns, crushed

2 tbsp Dijon mustard

4 x 150g (5oz) sirloin steaks

Salt-baked New Potatoes (see Cook's Tip) and cherry tomatoes to serve

fresh oregano sprigs to garnish

For the aïoli

2 garlic cloves, crushed

200ml (7fl oz) mayonnaise

2 tbsp lemon juice

salt and ground black pepper

1 Mix together the garlic, olive oil, crushed peppercorns and mustard. Spread the mixture on both sides of the steaks and leave to marinate for at least 15 minutes or overnight.

2 To make the aïoli, mix the garlic with the mayonnaise, lemon juice and salt and pepper. Cover and chill until ready to serve.

3 Preheat the barbecue, grill or griddle. Cook the steaks for 3–4 minutes on each side. Allow to rest in a warm place for 5 minutes before serving. Serve with salt-baked new potatoes and cherry tomatoes, and garnish with oregano sprigs. Serve the aïoli in a separate bowl.

Preparation Time: 15 minutes, plus minimum 15 minutes marinating

Cooking Time: 8 minutes

Serves: 4

Calories Per Serving: 607

Grilled Chicken with Pesto Butter

4 skinless, boneless chicken breasts

75g (3oz) butter, softened

3 tbsp pesto

lemon juice to sprinkle

salt and ground black pepper

tomato salad, new potatoes tossed with chopped parsley, and lemon wedges to serve

1 Make three or four deep cuts on each side of the chicken breasts. Season well with salt and pepper.

2 Put the butter into a bowl and gradually work in the pesto. Spread half of the pesto butter over the chicken and sprinkle with a little lemon juice.

3 Preheat the grill. Lay the chicken breasts on the grill rack and grill for about 10 minutes. Turn the chicken over, spread with the remaining pesto butter and sprinkle with a little more lemon juice. Grill for about 10 minutes or until cooked through.

4 Serve the chicken on warmed plates, with any pan juices poured over, with tomato salad, potatoes and lemon wedges.

Preparation Time: 10 minutes

Cooking Time: 20–30 minutes

Serves: 4

Calories Per Serving: 340

Chinese Spare Ribs

10 tbsp hoisin sauce

3 tbsp tomato ketchup

1 garlic clove, crushed

2 x 10-bone baby rack of ribs (available from butchers), cut into individual ribs

salt and ground black pepper

1 Put the hoisin sauce, ketchup and garlic in a large shallow dish. Season with salt and pepper and stir everything together until combined.

2 Add the ribs and toss to coat, spooning over the marinade to cover completely. You can either cook the ribs immediately or, if you have time, cover and chill them for 2 hours or overnight.

3 Preheat the barbecue or grill until medium-hot. Alternatively, preheat the oven to 200°C (180°C fan oven) mark 6. Lift the ribs from the marinade and barbecue or grill for 10–12 minutes on each side, or roast in the oven for 45 minutes.

Preparation Time: 5 minutes, plus 2 hours marinating (optional)

Cooking Time: 20–45 minutes

Serves: 4

Calories Per Serving: 310

Cook's Tip

Toasting the cashew nuts in a dry frying pan before adding them to the salad brings out their flavour, giving them an intense, nutty taste and a wonderful golden colour.

Orange and Chicken Salad

50g (2oz) cashew nuts

zest and juice of 2 oranges

2 tbsp marmalade

1 tbsp honey

1 tbsp oyster sauce

400g (14oz) roast chicken, shredded

a handful of chopped raw vegetables, such as cucumber, carrot, red and yellow pepper and Chinese leaves

1 Toast the cashew nuts in a dry frying pan and cook for 2–3 minutes until golden. Tip into a large serving bowl.

2 To make the dressing, put the orange zest and juice into the frying pan with the marmalade, honey and oyster sauce. Bring to the boil, stirring, then simmer for 2–3 minutes until slightly thickened.

3 Add the roast chicken to the serving bowl with the chopped raw vegetables. Pour the dressing over the salad, toss everything together and serve immediately.

Preparation Time: 15 minutes

Cooking Time: 10 minutes

Serves: 4

Calories Per Serving: 252

225g (8oz) piece salami, chorizo or garlic sausage, sliced or roughly chopped

50g (2oz) slightly stale sourdough bread (crusts removed), roughly chopped

8 large eggs

2 spring onions, finely chopped

1 small bunch chives, finely chopped, plus extra to garnish

ground black pepper

green salad to serve

Spanish Omelette

1 Heat a large, 28cm (11in), heavy-based frying pan, add the sausage pieces and fry over a low heat until the fat begins to run. Increase the heat and cook the sausage until golden and crisp. Remove from the pan (leaving the fat in the pan) and set aside. Add the bread to the pan and fry until it's also golden and crisp. Remove the pan from the heat, mix the croûtons with the cooked sausage and keep warm.

2 In a bowl, beat together the eggs, spring onions and chives, then season with pepper. Heat the pan used for the salami and bread. When very hot, add the egg mixture, allowing the liquid to spread across the base of the pan. Cook for 2 minutes, then, using a spatula, draw the cooked edges into the centre, tilting the pan so the mixture runs into the gaps.

3 When the omelette is almost set, reduce the heat and spoon the salami and croûton mixture evenly over the top. Cook for a further 30 seconds, then cut the omelette into four wedges. Sprinkle with chives and serve with a green salad.

Preparation Time: 5 minutes

Cooking Time: 15 minutes

Serves: 4

Calories Per Serving: 466

Moroccan Spiced Chicken Kebabs

2 tbsp olive oil

15g (½oz) flat-leafed parsley

1 garlic clove

½ tsp paprika

1 tsp ground cumin

grated zest and juice of 1 lemon

4 skinless, boneless chicken breasts, cut into bite-size chunks

1 Put the olive oil in a blender and add the parsley, garlic, paprika, cumin, lemon zest and juice. Whiz to make a paste.

2 Put the chicken in a shallow dish and add the spice paste, then rub in and leave to marinate for at least 20 minutes.

3 Preheat the barbecue or grill. Soak four wooden skewers in water for 20 minutes.

4 Thread the marinated chicken on to the skewers and grill for 10–12 minutes, turning every now and then, until cooked through.

Preparation Time: 10 minutes, plus minimum 20 minutes marinating

Cooking Time: 10–12 minutes

Serves: 4

Calories Per Serving: 189

Pasta and Pastrami Salad

150g (5oz) cooked pasta, cooled

50g (2oz) pastrami, diced

2 tomatoes, chopped

½ cucumber, chopped

2 tbsp freshly chopped parsley

75g (3oz) red onion, finely chopped

For the dressing

3 tbsp olive oil

1 tbsp white wine vinegar

½ tsp wholegrain or Dijon mustard

salt and ground black pepper

1 Combine all the ingredients for the salad in a salad bowl.

2 Put the dressing ingredients into a screw-topped jar and shake to combine. Pour on to the salad and toss, then serve.

Preparation Time: 10 minutes

Cooking Time: 20 minutes

Serves: 2

Calories Per Serving: 144

Seared Beef Salad

1 tbsp sunflower oil

4 rump steaks

125g (4oz) crème fraîche

3 tbsp horseradish

a squeeze of lemon juice

100g (3½oz) baby leaf spinach

150g (5oz) radishes, sliced

8 cherry tomatoes, halved

225g (8oz) cooked new potatoes, sliced

salt and ground black pepper

1 Heat a frying pan over a high heat until hot. Add the sunflower oil and turn the heat down to medium. Season the steaks, then cook for 1½ minutes on each side for rare or 2 minutes on each side for medium, depending on the thickness of the slices. Cover loosely with foil and leave to rest for 5 minutes, then carve into thin slices.

2 Mix the crème fraîche with the horseradish, lemon juice and 1 tbsp warm water.

3 Arrange the beef slices in four bowls. Scatter with the spinach, radishes, cherry tomatoes and sliced potatoes. Drizzle with the horseradish sauce and serve.

Preparation Time: 10 minutes

Cooking Time: 3–4 minutes, plus 5 minutes resting

Serves: 4

Calories Per Serving: 385

2 x 200g packs roast chicken

250g (9oz) baby leaf spinach

55g pack crisp bacon, broken into small pieces

For the dressing

grated zest of 1 lemon and 4 tbsp lemon juice

1 tsp caster sugar

1 tsp Dijon mustard

175ml (6fl oz) lemon-infused olive oil

4 tbsp freshly chopped basil

salt and ground black pepper

Basil and Lemon Chicken

1 To make the dressing, put the lemon zest and juice, caster sugar, Dijon mustard and olive oil into a small bowl and season with salt and pepper. Whisk thoroughly together and add the basil.

2 Remove any bones from the roast chicken, leave the skin attached and slice into five or six pieces. Arrange the sliced chicken in a dish and pour the dressing over, then cover and leave to marinate for at least 15 minutes.

3 Just before serving, lift the chicken from the dressing and put to one side.

4 Put the spinach in a large bowl, pour the dressing over and toss together. Arrange the chicken on top of the spinach and sprinkle with the bacon. Serve immediately.

Preparation Time: 15 minutes, plus minimum 15 minutes marinating

Serves: 4

Calories Per Serving: 331 calories

Cook's Tip

Instead of the spring onion butter, brush 4 spring onions per person lightly with oil and barbecue or grill for 5 minutes. Squeeze some fresh lime juice on top (saves 30 calories per serving).

2 garlic cloves, crushed

2 small red chillies, finely chopped (including seeds) (see page 17)

1 tsp ground allspice

2 tbsp dark rum

2 tbsp tomato ketchup

4 pork steaks, each weighing about 200g (7oz)

50g (2oz) butter, softened

2 spring onions, thinly sliced

4 corn cobs

salt and ground black pepper

Jamaican-spiced Pork Steaks

1 Mix together the garlic, chillies, allspice, rum and tomato ketchup. Brush all over the pork steaks, cover and chill for at least 30 minutes or overnight.

2 Mix the butter with the spring onions and plenty of black pepper; put to one side or cover and chill overnight.

3 Preheat the barbecue or grill. Cook the corn cobs in lightly salted boiling water for 2 minutes. Drain well, then barbecue or grill until cooked and beginning to char – about 4–5 minutes. Barbecue or grill the pork for about 5 minutes on each side until cooked through. Serve with the corn, smothered in spring onion butter.

Preparation Time: 20 minutes, plus minimum 30 minutes marinating

Cooking Time: 10 minutes

Serves: 4

Calories Per Serving: 355

Cook's Tip

Vine leaves preserved in brine are sold in large supermarkets and good delis.

Moroccan Lamb Kebabs

12 large vine leaves

3 garlic cloves, roughly chopped

1 onion, roughly chopped

½ tsp each ground coriander, ground cumin, sweet paprika and ground ginger

1kg (2¼lb) minced lamb

3 tbsp each freshly chopped mint and coriander

olive oil

salt and ground black pepper

pitta bread, tzatziki, hummus and tomato salad to serve

1 Preheat the barbecue to medium-hot. Soak six long wooden skewers in water for 30 minutes. Rinse the vine leaves and dry on kitchen paper.

2 Put the garlic, onion and spices in a food processor and whiz to form a paste. Add the minced lamb and herbs and pulse again until mixed. Season with salt and pepper. Divide into 12 and, with damp hands, roll into long sausage shapes. Wrap each sausage in a vine leaf and skewer lengthways through the middle, putting two kebabs on each skewer. Brush generously with olive oil and place side by side across the grill rack.

3 Barbecue for 4–5 minutes on each side. Serve with toasted pitta bread, tzatziki, hummus and a tomato salad.

Preparation Time: 40 minutes

Cooking Time: 8–10 minutes

Serves: 6

Calories Per Serving: 316

Chicken, Avocado and Peanut Salad

2 roast chicken breasts, about 250g (9oz) total weight, skinned and sliced

75g (3oz) watercress

2 tbsp cider vinegar

1 tsp English ready-made mustard

5 tbsp groundnut oil

1 large ripe avocado, halved, stoned, peeled and thickly sliced

50g (2oz) roasted salted peanuts, roughly chopped

salt and ground black pepper

1 Arrange the sliced chicken on top of the watercress, cover with clingfilm and chill until ready to serve.

2 Put the cider vinegar, mustard and groundnut oil together in a bowl, season with salt and pepper and whisk together. Add the avocado and gently toss in the dressing, making sure each slice of avocado is well coated.

3 Just before serving, spoon the avocado and dressing over the chicken and watercress. Sprinkle with the chopped peanuts and serve immediately.

Preparation Time: 15 minutes, plus chilling

Serves: 4

Calories Per Serving: 335

6 duck legs, about 200g (7oz) each

2 fresh thyme sprigs

1 tsp peppercorns

2 bay leaves

2 tsp salt

125g (4oz) kumquats

125g (4oz) pecan nuts, toasted

finely grated zest and juice of 2 oranges

225g (8oz) cranberries

125g (4oz) caster sugar

4 tbsp white wine vinegar

9 tbsp sunflower oil

3 tbsp walnut oil

salt and ground black pepper

frisée leaves to serve

Crispy Duck Salad

1 Preheat the oven to 180°C (160°C fan oven) mark 4. Put the duck into a large flameproof casserole, cover with cold water and bring to the boil. Simmer for 10 minutes, skim and add the thyme, peppercorns, bay leaves and salt. Cook in the oven for 45 minutes–1 hour until tender. Cool quickly in the liquid and chill overnight.

2 Toast the nuts lightly under a grill. Put the orange zest, 200ml (7fl oz) orange juice, the cranberries and sugar in a frying pan. Bring to the boil and simmer for 5 minutes or until the cranberries are tender. Strain the juice into a pan, reserving the berries. Bring the juice to the boil and bubble until syrupy. Add the cranberries.

3 Whisk the vinegar and oils in a bowl. Season with salt and pepper. Quarter the kumquats and add to the cranberry mixture with the oil and vinegar dressing and the pecan nuts.

4 Skim the fat from the jellied duck and set aside. Cut the duck into thick shreds, leaving the skin on. Heat 1 tbsp of the reserved duck fat in a non-stick frying pan and fry half the duck for 5 minutes or until crisp and brown. Keep warm and repeat with the remaining duck. Toss the duck with the cranberry mixture and serve with salad leaves.

Preparation Time: 10 minutes, plus cooling and overnight chilling

Cooking Time: 1½ hours

Serves: 8

Calories Per Serving: 655

Try Something Different

For an even more nutritious salad, add a few pumpkin seeds or sunflower seeds, or a handful of sprouted seeds such as alfalfa.
For extra bite, add a little finely chopped red chilli.
For extra sweetness, add some strips of red pepper.
For extra flavour, add some freshly chopped coriander or watercress or torn basil leaves.

100g (3½oz) shredded roast chicken, skin discarded

1 carrot, chopped

1 celery stick, chopped

¼ cucumber, chopped

handful of ripe cherry tomatoes, chopped

1 tbsp hummus

¼ lemon to serve

Easy Chicken Salad

1 Put the chicken into a shallow bowl. Add the carrot, celery, cucumber and cherry tomatoes.

2 Top with the hummus and serve with lemon for squeezing over the salad.

Preparation Time: 10 minutes

Serves: 1

Calories Per Serving: 323

Marinated Beef and Vegetable Stir-fry

2 rump steaks, about 175g (6oz) each, trimmed

1 tsp vegetable oil

300g pack straight-to-wok noodles

1 red pepper, seeded and thinly sliced

300g (11oz) cabbage, shredded

2 carrots, cut into matchsticks

150g (5oz) shiitake mushrooms, sliced

300g (11oz) bean sprouts

For the sauce

1 red chilli, finely chopped (see page 17)

1 garlic clove, finely chopped

2 tbsp soy sauce

2 tbsp sweet chilli sauce

juice of 1 lime

1 First, make the sauce. Put all the sauce ingredients in a large shallow bowl and mix well. Add the steaks and turn to coat. Cover and chill in the refrigerator for up to 24 hours, if you like.

2 Heat the vegetable oil in a wok or large frying pan over a high heat. Remove the steaks from the sauce, reserving the sauce, and cook them for 1–2 minutes on each side. Remove from the pan and set aside.

3 Add the noodles, red pepper, cabbage, carrots and mushrooms to the pan and stir-fry over a high heat for 2–3 minutes. Add the bean sprouts and the reserved sauce and stir-fry for a further 2–3 minutes.

4 Thinly slice the steak and add it to the pan. Toss everything together and serve immediately.

Preparation Time: 15 minutes, plus up to 24 hours chilling

Cooking Time: about 10 minutes

Serves: 4

Calories Per Serving: 543

Try Something Different

For a vegetarian alternative, replace the ham with 150g (5oz) Gruyère or Cheddar cheese, cubed.
Spicy cumin dressing: mix together 2 tbsp red wine vinegar, 1 tsp ground cumin, a pinch of caster sugar and 5 tbsp olive oil. Season to taste.

Apple, Chicory, Ham and Pecan Salad

450g (1lb) fennel bulb, halved

2 large Braeburn or Cox's apples, about 450g (1lb), quartered, cored and sliced

75g (3oz) shelled pecan nuts

300g (11oz) cooked ham, cut into wide strips

1 chicory head, divided into leaves

fresh flat-leafed parsley sprigs to garnish

For the poppy seed dressing

1 tsp clear honey

2 tsp German or Dijon mustard

3 tbsp cider vinegar

9 tbsp vegetable oil

2 tsp poppy seeds

salt and ground black pepper

1 To make the dressing, whisk together the honey, mustard, cider vinegar and seasoning in a small bowl. Whisk in the vegetable oil, then the poppy seeds. Put to one side.

2 Remove and discard the centre core from the fennel and slice the fennel thinly lengthways. Place the fennel, apples, nuts, ham and chicory in a large serving bowl. Toss with the dressing and adjust the seasoning if necessary. Garnish with parsley sprigs and serve immediately.

Preparation Time: 15 minutes

Serves: 6

Calories Per Serving: 340

Get Ahead

Complete the recipe to the end of step 2, cover and chill separately overnight.
To use Complete the recipe.

350g (12oz) smoked chicken or cooked chicken breast, skinned and cut into long strips

2 oranges

2 large chicory heads, roughly sliced

50g (2oz) pecan nuts or walnuts, toasted and roughly chopped

fresh tarragon sprigs to garnish

For the orange and tarragon dressing

grated zest and juice of 2 oranges

2 tbsp white wine vinegar

1 tsp caster sugar

5 tbsp olive oil

3 tbsp freshly chopped tarragon

1 large egg yolk

salt and ground black pepper

Zesty Orange, Chicken and Tarragon Salad

1 To make the dressing, whisk all the ingredients together in a small bowl.

2 Put the chicken strips in a bowl, spoon over the dressing, cover and chill for at least 1 hour.

3 Remove and discard the peel and pith from the oranges, then cut into slices.

4 Place a layer of chicory in a large flat salad bowl and spoon the chicken and dressing over. Scatter on the orange slices and nuts, garnish with tarragon sprigs and serve.

Preparation Time: 15 minutes, plus minimum 1 hour chilling

Serves: 4

Calories Per Serving: 252

Try Something Different

Use 400g (14oz) pork escalope cut into strips instead of beef. Cook for 5 minutes before removing from the pan at step 2.

2 tbsp soy sauce

2 tbsp Worcestershire sauce

2 tsp tomato purée

juice of ½ lemon

1 tbsp sesame seeds

1 garlic clove, crushed

400g (14oz) rump steak, sliced

1 tbsp vegetable oil

3 small pak choi, chopped

1 bunch spring onions, sliced

freshly cooked egg noodles or tagliatelle to serve

Sesame Beef

1 In a bowl, mix together the soy sauce, Worcestershire sauce, tomato purée, lemon juice, sesame seeds and garlic. Add the steak and toss to coat.

2 Heat the vegetable oil in a large wok or non-stick frying pan until hot. Add the steak and sear well. Remove from the wok and set aside.

3 Add any sauce from the bowl to the wok and heat for 1 minute. Add the pak choi, spring onions and steak, and stir-fry for 5 minutes. Add freshly cooked and drained noodles, toss and serve immediately.

Preparation Time: 10 minutes

Cooking Time: 10 minutes

Serves: 4

Calories Per Serving: 207

Rice and Red Pepper Stir-fry

75g (3oz) long-grain rice

200ml (7fl oz) hot vegetable stock

2 tsp vegetable oil

½ onion, thinly sliced

2 rashers of streaky bacon, chopped

1 small red pepper, seeded and cut into chunks

a handful of frozen peas

a dash of Worcestershire sauce

1 Put the rice in a pan and pour over the hot stock. Cover, bring to the boil and simmer for 10 minutes or until the rice is tender and the liquid has been absorbed.

2 Meanwhile, heat the vegetable oil in a wok or large frying pan over a medium heat. Add the onion and fry for 5 minutes. Add the bacon and red pepper and fry for a further 5 minutes or until the bacon is crisp.

3 Stir the cooked rice and the peas into the onion mixture and cook, stirring occasionally, for 2–3 minutes until the rice and peas are hot. Add a dash of Worcestershire sauce and serve immediately.

Preparation Time: 5 minutes

Cooking Time: 15 minutes

Serves: 4

Calories Per Serving: 157

4 duck breast fillets, about 175g (6oz) each

1½ tbsp clear honey

3 tbsp vegetable oil

1 bunch spring onions, cut into 2.5cm (1in) lengths

1 large green pepper, seeded and cut into thin strips

225g (8oz) mangetouts

2 garlic cloves, crushed

2–3 good pinches of Chinese five-spice powder

3 tbsp caster sugar

3 tbsp dark soy sauce

3 tbsp wine vinegar

16 water chestnuts, sliced

40g (1½oz) toasted cashew nuts

salt

Crispy Duck with Mangetouts

1 Preheat the oven to 180°C (160°C fan oven) mark 4. Prick the duck skin all over with a skewer or fork and rub well with salt. Put the breasts, skin side up, on a rack or trivet in a roasting tin and cook in the oven, uncovered, for 15 minutes.

2 Remove the duck breasts from the oven and brush the skins with honey. Return them to the oven and cook for a further 5–10 minutes or until the duck is cooked through. Leave to cool, then cut into strips.

3 Heat the vegetable oil in a wok or large frying pan. Add the spring onions, green pepper, mangetouts, garlic and five-spice powder and stir-fry for 2 minutes. Add the caster sugar, soy sauce, wine vinegar and duck strips and toss in the sauce to heat through and glaze. Add the water chestnuts and cook until heated through.

4 Sprinkle with toasted cashew nuts and serve immediately.

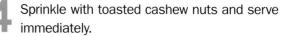

Preparation Time: 15 minutes, plus cooling

Cooking Time: about 30 minutes

Serves: 6

Calories Per Serving: 308

Try Something Different

Use pork fillet instead of beef, trimmed of fat and cut into thin slices.

1 tsp chilli oil

1 tbsp each tamari (wheat-free Japanese soy sauce) and runny honey

1 garlic clove, crushed

1 large red chilli, halved, seeded and chopped (see page 17)

400g (14oz) lean beef, cut into strips

1 tsp sunflower oil

1 broccoli head, thinly sliced

200g (7oz) mangetouts, halved

1 red pepper, halved, seeded and cut into strips

rice to serve

Sweet Chilli Beef Stir-fry

1 Pour the chilli oil into a medium-sized shallow bowl. Add the tamari, honey, garlic and chilli and stir well. Add the strips of beef and toss in the marinade.

2 Heat the sunflower oil in a wok over a high heat until it is very hot. Cook the strips of beef in two batches, for 3–4 minutes, or until just cooked through, then remove them from the wok and set aside. Wipe the wok with kitchen paper to remove any residue.

3 Add the broccoli, mangetouts, red pepper and 2 tbsp water and stir-fry for 5–6 minutes until starting to soften. Return the beef to the wok to heat through. Serve with rice.

Preparation Time: 10 minutes

Cooking Time: 10–15 minutes

Serves: 4

Calories Per Serving: 273

Thai Poached Chicken

2 limes, halved

1.4kg (3lb) chicken

a knob of butter

2 lemongrass stalks, crushed

450ml (¾ pint) dry white wine

450ml (¾ pint) chicken stock

1 small bunch freshly chopped coriander

salt and ground black pepper

rice and vegetables to serve

1 Preheat the oven to 200°C (180°C fan oven) mark 6. Put 2 lime halves into the cavity of the chicken. Rub the chicken with the butter, and season with salt and pepper. Put into a flameproof casserole.

2 Add the lemongrass and remaining lime to the casserole. Pour in the white wine and stock. Cover and cook in the oven for 1 hour. Remove the lid and cook for a further 30 minutes. Scatter the coriander over and serve with rice and vegetables.

Preparation Time: 5 minutes

Cooking Time: 1½ hours

Serves: 4

Calories Per Serving: 579

Try Something Different

Use 450g (1lb) chicken or turkey strips instead of pork.

Pork and Noodle Stir-fry

1 tbsp sesame oil

5cm (2in) piece fresh root ginger, peeled and grated

2 tbsp soy sauce

1 tbsp fish sauce

½ red chilli, finely chopped (see page 17)

450g (1lb) stir-fry pork strips

2 red peppers, halved, seeded and roughly chopped

250g (9oz) baby sweetcorn, halved lengthways

200g (7oz) sugarsnap peas, halved

300g (11oz) bean sprouts

250g (9oz) rice noodles

1 Put the sesame oil into a large bowl. Add the ginger, soy sauce, fish sauce, chilli and pork strips. Mix well and leave to marinate for 10 minutes.

2 Heat a large wok until hot. Lift the pork out of the marinade with a slotted spoon and add to the pan. Stir-fry over a high heat for 5 minutes. Add the red peppers, corn, sugarsnap peas, bean sprouts and remaining marinade, and stir-fry for a further 2–3 minutes until the pork is cooked.

3 Meanwhile, bring a large pan of water to the boil and cook the noodles according to the packet instructions.

4 Drain the noodles, tip into the wok and toss together, then serve immediately.

Preparation Time: 10 minutes, plus 10 minutes marinating

Cooking Time: 7–8 minutes

Serves: 4

Calories Per Serving: 500

Try Something Different

Use flageolet beans or other canned beans instead of mixed beans and garnish with fresh basil or oregano.

One-pan Chicken with Tomatoes

4 chicken thighs

1 red onion, sliced

400g can chopped tomatoes with herbs

400g can mixed beans, drained and rinsed

2 tsp balsamic vinegar

freshly chopped flat-leafed parsley to garnish

1 Heat a non-stick pan and fry the chicken thighs, skin side down, until golden. Turn over and fry for 5 minutes.

2 Add the onion and fry for 5 minutes. Add the tomatoes, mixed beans and balsamic vinegar. Cover and simmer for 10–12 minutes until piping hot. Garnish with parsley and serve immediately.

Preparation Time: 5 minutes

Cooking Time: 20–25 minutes

Serves: 4

Calories Per Serving: 238

Try Something Different

Replace the pinenuts with walnuts.

125g (4oz) streaky bacon rashers, de-rinded and cut into small, neat pieces (lardons)

1 shallot, finely chopped

120g bag mixed baby salad leaves

1 ripe avocado

50g (2oz) pinenuts

4 tbsp olive oil

4 tbsp red wine vinegar

salt and ground black pepper

Bacon, Avocado and Pinenut Salad

1 Put the lardons into a frying pan over a medium heat for 1–2 minutes until the fat starts to run. Add the shallot and fry gently for about 5 minutes until golden.

2 Meanwhile, divide the salad leaves among four serving plates. Halve and stone the avocado, then peel, and slice the flesh. Arrange on the salad leaves.

3 Add the pinenuts, olive oil and wine vinegar to the frying pan and let bubble for 1 minute. Season with salt and pepper.

4 Tip the bacon, pinenuts and dressing over the salad and serve immediately, while still warm.

Preparation Time: 5 minutes

Cooking Time: 7 minutes

Serves: 4

Calories Per Serving: 352

Try Something Different

Use mixed beans, red kidney beans or chickpeas instead of cannellini beans.
Replace the turkey with cooked chicken.

2 tbsp roughly chopped fresh tarragon

2 tbsp roughly chopped flat-leafed parsley

1 tbsp olive oil

2 tbsp crème fraîche

200ml (7fl oz) mayonnaise

juice of ½ lemon

450g (1lb) cooked turkey, cut into bite-size pieces

400g can cannellini beans, drained and rinsed

50g (2oz) sunblush or sun-dried tomatoes, roughly chopped

salt and ground black pepper

finely sliced spring onion to garnish

For the shallot dressing

2 tbsp sunflower oil

1 tsp walnut oil

2 tsp red wine vinegar

1 small shallot, very finely chopped

a pinch of caster sugar

Tarragon Turkey and Bean Salad

1 Put the herbs in a food processor and add the olive oil. Whiz until the herbs are chopped. Add the crème fraîche, mayonnaise and lemon juice to the processor and season with salt and pepper, then whiz until well combined. Alternatively, chop the herbs by hand, mix with the olive oil, then beat in the crème fraîche, mayonnaise, lemon juice and seasoning. Toss the turkey with the herb dressing in a large bowl and put to one side.

2 To make the shallot dressing, whisk the ingredients together in a small bowl and season with salt and pepper.

3 Tip the cannellini beans into a bowl, toss with the shallot dressing and season well. Arrange the cannellini beans on a serving dish. Top the beans with the dressed turkey and the tomatoes, garnish with spring onion and serve.

Preparation Time: 15–20 minutes

Serves: 4

Calories Per Serving: 719

Cook's Tip

Paprika potatoes: cut 550g (1¼lb) scrubbed potatoes into wedges and cook in a pan of boiling water for 5 minutes. Drain, rinse, then toss in 3 tbsp olive oil, 2 tbsp paprika and plenty of salt and pepper. Barbecue or grill for 10 minutes until golden and cooked through.

Apricot and Gin-glazed Gammon

4 tbsp gin

6 tbsp apricot jam

4 x 225g (8oz) gammon steaks

75g (3oz) butter, softened

2 tbsp chopped flat-leafed parsley, plus extra sprigs to garnish

50g (2oz) ready-to-eat dried apricots, finely chopped

lemon juice

ground black pepper

Paprika Potatoes (see Cook's Tip) to serve

1 Mix the gin and jam together and cover the gammon steaks with the mixture. Set aside for 10 minutes, or cover and chill overnight. Mix together the butter, parsley, apricots and lemon juice to taste. Season with pepper, cover and chill.

2 Preheat the barbecue or grill. Cook the gammon steaks for 2–3 minutes on each side, then serve immediately, topped with the apricot butter, garnished with parsley sprigs, and with paprika potatoes.

Preparation Time: 10 minutes, plus 10 minutes marinating

Cooking Time: 6 minutes

Serves: 4

Calories Per Serving: 710

Grilled Chicken with Mango Salsa

4 chicken breasts

juice of ½ lime

oil-water spray

salt and ground black pepper

rocket leaves to serve

For the salsa

1 mango, peeled, stoned and diced

1 small head of fennel, trimmed and diced

1 fresh chilli, seeded and finely diced (see page 17)

1 tbsp balsamic vinegar

juice of ½ lime

2 tbsp freshly chopped flat-leafed parsley

2 tbsp freshly chopped mint

1 Put the chicken on a grill pan and season generously with salt and pepper. Pour over the lime juice and spray with the oil-water. Grill for 8–10 minutes on each side until cooked through and the juices run clear when pierced with a skewer. Set aside.

2 Combine all the salsa ingredients in a bowl and season generously with salt and pepper. Spoon alongside the chicken and serve with rocket leaves.

Preparation Time: 10 minutes

Cooking Time: 20 minutes

Serves: 4

Calories Per Serving: 288

Get Ahead

Make the croûtons, then cool and place in an airtight container for up to one week. Grill the bacon, then cool, cover and chill for up to one day. **To use** Place the croûtons on a baking sheet and warm in the oven at 200°C (180°C fan oven) mark 6 for 5 minutes. Complete the recipe.

75ml (2½fl oz) olive oil

75g (3oz) ciabatta bread, cut into cubes

½ tsp sea salt flakes

6 rashers of streaky bacon

2 Little Gem lettuces, broken into leaves

25g (1oz) Parmesan, pared into shavings with a vegetable peeler

25g (1oz) rocket leaves

50g (2oz) marinated fresh anchovies

75ml (3fl oz) Caesar dressing

Bacon, Parmesan and Anchovy Salad

1 Put half the olive oil in a frying pan and heat gently until a cube of bread sizzles. Add half the cubed bread and toss over the heat for 2–3 minutes or until golden. Remove with a slotted spoon and drain on kitchen paper. Repeat with the rest of the oil and bread, toss the croûtons in the salt and leave to cool.

2 Grill the bacon for 3–4 minutes on each side until golden and crisp. Drain and cool on kitchen paper, then roughly chop.

3 Toss the lettuce and Parmesan with the croûtons, bacon pieces, rocket leaves and anchovies. Drizzle the salad with the dressing before serving.

Preparation Time: 15 minutes, plus cooling

Cooking Time: 15 minutes

Serves: 8

Calories Per Serving: 339

2 tbsp mango chutney

juice of ½ lemon

1 tbsp olive oil

2 tsp mild curry powder

1 tsp paprika

350g (12oz) skinless, boneless chicken breast, cut into thick strips

200g (7oz) quinoa

1 cucumber, roughly chopped

½ bunch spring onions, sliced

50g (2oz) ready-to-eat dried apricots, sliced

2 tbsp chopped fresh mint, basil or tarragon

Mild Spiced Chicken and Quinoa

1 Put the chutney, lemon juice, ½ tbsp olive oil, curry powder and paprika into a bowl and mix together. Add the chicken and toss to coat.

2 Cook the quinoa in boiling water for 10–12 minutes until tender (or according to the packet instructions). Drain thoroughly. Put into a bowl, then stir in the cucumber, spring onions, apricots, herbs and remaining oil.

3 Put the chicken and marinade into a pan and fry over a high heat for 2–3 minutes, then add 150ml (¼ pint) water. Bring to the boil, then simmer for 5 minutes or until the chicken is cooked. Serve with the quinoa.

Preparation Time: 15 minutes

Cooking Time: 20 minutes

Serves: 4

Calories Per Serving: 268

Freezing Tip

Complete the recipe to the end of step 1, place the patties on a tray to freeze, then wrap, label and freeze for up to one month.
To use Thaw at cool room temperature. Complete the recipe.

Spiced Lamb in Pitta

1 small green pepper, seeded and chopped

½ small onion, chopped

3 garlic cloves

2 tsp ground cumin

3 tbsp olive oil

1 tbsp freshly chopped mint

550g (1¼lb) lean minced lamb

450g (1lb) very ripe tomatoes, chopped

2 tbsp freshly chopped flat-leafed parsley

4 large pitta breads

salt and ground black pepper

Greek yogurt to serve

mint sprigs to garnish

1 Put the chopped pepper and onion in a food processor with the garlic, cumin and olive oil, and pulse to form a coarse paste. Add the chopped mint. Mix together the paste and the minced lamb, season with salt and pepper and shape into 16 patties. Chill for 30 minutes or overnight.

2 Put the tomatoes in a bowl, stir in the parsley and season with salt and pepper.

3 Preheat the barbecue, griddle or grill. Cook the lamb patties for 4–5 minutes on each side. Warm the pitta breads, wrap into a cone and secure with a cocktail stick. Fill each with four lamb patties and spoon on a drizzle of yogurt. Serve with the tomatoes and garnish with mint sprigs.

Preparation Time: 20 minutes, plus 30 minutes chilling

Cooking Time: 8–10 minutes

Serves: 4

Calories Per Serving: 550

Try Something Different

Other vegetables are just as good in this dish: try pak choi, button mushrooms, carrots cut into matchsticks, or baby sweetcorn.

Quick Chicken Stir-fry

1 tsp groundnut oil

300g (11oz) skinless, boneless chicken breasts, sliced

4 spring onions, chopped

200g (7oz) medium rice noodles

100g (3½oz) mangetouts

200g (7oz) purple sprouting broccoli, chopped

2–3 tbsp sweet chilli sauce

freshly chopped coriander and lime wedges (optional) to garnish

1 Heat the groundnut oil in a wok or large frying pan and add the chicken and spring onions. Stir-fry over a high heat for 5–6 minutes until the chicken is golden.

2 Meanwhile, soak the rice noodles in boiling water for 4 minutes or according to the packet instructions.

3 Add the mangetouts, broccoli and chilli sauce to the chicken. Continue to stir-fry for 4 minutes.

4 Drain the noodles and add them to the pan. Toss everything together. Scatter the chopped coriander over the top and serve with lime wedges to squeeze over, if you like.

Preparation Time: 10 minutes

Cooking Time: 12 minutes

Serves: 4

Calories Per Serving: 316

Cook's Tip

Butterflied lamb is a leg of lamb with the bone removed. Most butchers will do this for you.

Butterflied Leg of Lamb

1 leg of lamb, about 2.3kg (5lb) boned

175ml (6fl oz) extra virgin olive oil, plus extra to brush

1 tbsp dried oregano

3 tbsp fresh thyme leaves

2 tbsp freshly chopped flat-leafed parsley

6 garlic cloves, finely chopped

150ml (¼ pint) balsamic vinegar

zest and juice of 2 small really ripe lemons

new potatoes and mixed leaf salad to serve

1 Open out the meat, lay skin side down and trim away any excess fat. Make slits all over it to help the marinade penetrate the flesh. Place the lamb in a large glass dish big enough to take it in a single layer. Whisk the olive oil, herbs, garlic, balsamic vinegar, lemon zest and juice together in a small bowl and pour over the meat, rubbing well into the slits. Cover and leave to marinate overnight in the refrigerator.

2 Remove from the refrigerator an hour before barbecuing and put in a cool place. Preheat the barbecue to medium-hot. Lift from the marinade (don't throw it away) and barbecue for 35–40 minutes, turning frequently to ensure even cooking, and basting with the marinade from time to time. The meat should be slightly pink in the centre.

3 Remove from the heat, place on a board and cover loosely with foil. Leave to rest for 10 minutes and then carve across the width into long thin slices. Serve with minted new potatoes and a mixed leaf salad.

Preparation Time: 20 minutes, plus overnight marinating and resting

Cooking Time: 35–40 minutes

Serves: 8

Calories Per Serving: 509

Try Something Different

Replace the chicken with thinly sliced turkey escalopes.
Increase the spiciness by frying a chopped chilli with the garlic and ginger.

225g (8oz) fine egg noodles

about 2 tbsp vegetable oil

1 skinless, boneless chicken breast, cut into very thin strips

2.5cm (1in) piece fresh root ginger, peeled and finely chopped

1 garlic clove, finely chopped

1 red pepper, seeded and thinly sliced

4 spring onions, thinly sliced, plus extra to garnish

2 carrots, thinly sliced

125g (4oz) shiitake or button mushrooms, halved

a handful of bean sprouts (optional)

3 tbsp hoisin sauce

2 tbsp light soy sauce

1 tbsp chilli sauce

sesame seeds to garnish

Chicken with Vegetables and Noodles

1 Bring a large pan of water to the boil and cook the noodles for about 3 minutes or according to the packet instructions. Drain thoroughly and toss with a little of the vegetable oil to prevent them sticking together; set aside.

2 Heat the remaining oil in a wok or large frying pan. Add the chicken, ginger and garlic and cook over a very high heat until the chicken is browned on the outside and cooked right through, about 5 minutes.

3 Add all the vegetables to the pan and stir-fry over a high heat for about 2 minutes or until they are just cooked, but still crunchy.

4 Stir in the hoisin sauce, soy sauce and chilli sauce and mix well. Add the noodles, toss well to mix and cook for a couple of minutes until heated through. Serve immediately, sprinkled with shredded spring onion and sesame seeds.

Preparation Time: 10 minutes

Cooking Time: about 12 minutes

Serves: 2

Calories Per Serving: 584

Lamb Steaks with Mixed Bean Salad

150g (5oz) sunblush tomatoes in oil

1 garlic clove, crushed

2 rosemary sprigs

4 x 175g (6oz) leg of lamb steaks

½ small red onion, finely sliced

2 x 400g cans mixed beans, drained and rinsed

large handful of rocket leaves

salt and ground black pepper

1 Preheat the grill to high. Drain the sunblush tomatoes, reserving the oil. Put the garlic in a large, shallow dish with 1 tbsp oil from the tomatoes. Strip the leaves from the rosemary sprigs, snip into small pieces and add to the dish. Season with salt and pepper, then add the lamb and toss to coat.

2 Grill the lamb for 3–4 minutes on each side until cooked but still just pink. Meanwhile, roughly chop the tomatoes and put into a pan with the onion, beans, remaining rosemary, rocket leaves and a further 1 tbsp oil from the tomatoes. Warm through until the rocket starts to wilt. Serve the lamb steaks with the bean salad on warmed plates.

Preparation Time: 5 minutes

Cooking Time: 10 minutes

Serves: 4

Calories Per Serving: 545

Cook's Tip

Sunblush tomatoes are softer than the sun-dried version as they are not dried for as long.

Chilli Beef Noodle Salad

150g (5oz) dried rice noodles

juice of 1 lime

1 lemongrass stalk, outside leaves discarded, finely chopped

1 red chilli, seeded and chopped (see page 17)

2 tsp finely chopped fresh root ginger

2 garlic cloves, crushed

1 tbsp Thai fish sauce

3 tbsp extra virgin olive oil

50g (2oz) rocket leaves

125g (4oz) sliced cold roast beef

125g (4oz) sunblush tomatoes, chopped

salt and ground black pepper

1 Put the noodles in a large bowl and pour over boiling water to cover. Put to one side for 15 minutes.

2 Meanwhile, in a small bowl, whisk together the lime juice, lemongrass, chilli, ginger, garlic, fish sauce and olive oil. Season with salt and pepper.

3 While they are still warm, drain the noodles well, put in a large bowl and toss with the dressing. Allow to cool.

4 Just before serving, toss the rocket leaves, sliced beef and chopped tomatoes through the noodles.

Preparation Time: 15 minutes, plus 15 minutes soaking

Serves: 4

Calories Per Serving: 286

700g (1½lb) boned leg of lamb

75g (3oz) ready-to-eat dried apricots

150g (5oz) ready-to-eat dried figs

1 garlic clove, crushed

50g (2oz) spring onions, finely chopped

juice of 2 lemons

6 tbsp Greek yogurt

5 tbsp smooth peanut butter

2 tsp each ground coriander and cumin seeds

1 tsp ground fenugreek

½ tsp chilli powder

3 tbsp olive oil

salt and ground black pepper

225g (8oz) whole onions

2 large oranges

salad leaves to serve

Lamb, Orange and Apricot Kebabs

1 Trim the lamb and cut into large cubes, allowing about three pieces per skewer. Put the apricots and figs in a bowl; add enough water to cover completely, cover and chill.

2 In a large bowl, mix the garlic and spring onions with 8 tbsp lemon juice and all the remaining ingredients apart from the whole onions and oranges. Add the lamb to the marinade and stir to coat well. Cover and chill for at least 6 hours or overnight.

3 Preheat the barbecue and, if using wooden skewers, soak eight in water for 20 minutes. Quarter the onions, then separate the quarters into petals. Thickly slice the oranges. Thread the meat, onions, oranges, apricots and figs on to skewers.

4 Barbecue for 25–30 minutes or until the lamb is pink to the centre. Serve hot, with salad leaves.

Preparation Time: 45 minutes, plus minimum 6 hours marinating

Cooking Time: 25–30 minutes

Serves: 8

Calories Per Serving: 260

Fish and Seafood

Fast Fish Soup

1 leek, finely sliced

4 fat garlic cloves, crushed

3 celery sticks, finely sliced

1 small fennel bulb, finely sliced

1 red chilli, seeded and finely chopped (see page 17)

3 tbsp olive oil

50ml (2fl oz) white wine

about 750g (1½lb) mixed fish and shellfish, such as haddock, monkfish, salmon, raw shelled prawns and cleaned mussels

4 medium tomatoes, chopped

20g (¾oz) fresh thyme, finely chopped

salt and ground black pepper

1 Put the leek in a large pan and add the garlic, celery, fennel, chilli and olive oil. Cook over a medium heat for 5 minutes or until the vegetables are soft and beginning to colour.

2 Stir in 1.1 litres (2 pints) boiling water and the white wine. Bring to the boil, then simmer the soup, covered, for 5 minutes.

3 Meanwhile, cut the fish into large chunks. Add to the soup with the tomatoes and thyme. Continue simmering gently until the fish has just turned opaque. Add the prawns and simmer for 1 minute then add the mussels – if you're using them. As soon as all the mussels have opened, season the soup and ladle into warmed bowls. Discard any mussels that haven't opened. Serve immediately.

Preparation Time: 10 minutes

Cooking Time: 15 minutes

Serves: 4

Calories Per Serving: 269

Cook's Tip

Basmati rice is prized for its delicate fragrant flavour. Its long grains are firm and separate when cooked, not sticky, making it perfect for this tasty kedgeree.

Salmon and Coriander Kedgeree

1 tbsp olive oil

4 shallots, chopped

225g (8oz) basmati rice

450ml (¾ pint) hot fish stock

100g (3½oz) frozen peas

300g (11oz) hot-smoked salmon flakes

a handful of freshly chopped coriander

salt and ground black pepper

lime wedges to serve

1 Heat the olive oil in a large pan over a low heat and fry the shallots for 5 minutes or until soft. Add the rice and stir to mix everything together. Pour in the stock. Cover and cook for 10 minutes over a low heat until the rice is almost cooked and most of the liquid has been absorbed.

2 Add the peas and salmon and cook, uncovered, for 2–3 minutes until the peas are tender. Season with salt and pepper, scatter over the chopped coriander and serve with lime wedges to squeeze over.

Preparation Time: 5 minutes

Cooking Time: 20 minutes

Serves: 4

Calories Per Serving: 368

1 small butternut squash, peeled and cut into small cubes

½ red onion, finely sliced

2 garlic cloves, finely chopped

1 tbsp roughly chopped dill, plus extra sprigs to garnish

1 tbsp olive oil

4 thick haddock or salmon fillets, about 150g (5oz) each

125g (4oz) fresh spinach

salt and ground black pepper

lemon wedges and boiled new potatoes to serve

Baked Fish

1 Preheat the oven to 220°C (200°C fan) mark 7. Cut out four 40.5cm (16in) squares of foil.

2 Put the squash in a bowl. Add the onion, garlic, chopped dill and olive oil, and toss to coat. Season well with salt and pepper. Divide the vegetable mixture equally among the four squares of foil.

3 Top each pile of vegetables with a piece of fish. Season again, then bring the foil together and crimp the edges so that the fish and vegetables are completely enclosed. Put the parcels on a baking tray and roast for 15 minutes or until the fish is cooked through and the squash is just tender.

4 Carefully open each of the foil parcels and add the spinach. Close again and roast for a further 5 minutes or until the spinach has wilted. Garnish with dill sprigs and serve with lemon wedges to squeeze over the fish, and new potatoes.

Preparation Time: 10 minutes

Cooking Time: 20 minutes

Serves: 4

Calories Per Serving: 191

Cook's Tip

Laksa paste is a hot and spicy paste; you could use Thai curry paste instead.

Salmon Laksa Curry

1 tbsp olive oil

1 onion, thinly sliced

3 tbsp laksa paste (see Cook's Tip)

200ml (7fl oz) coconut milk

900ml (1½ pints) hot vegetable stock

200g (7oz) baby sweetcorn, halved lengthways

600g (1lb 5oz) piece skinless salmon fillet, cut into 1cm (½in) slices

225g (8oz) baby leaf spinach

250g (9oz) medium rice noodles

salt and ground black pepper

2 spring onions, sliced diagonally, 2 tbsp freshly chopped coriander and 1 lime, cut into wedges, to garnish

1 Heat the olive oil in a wok or large frying pan, then add the onion and fry over a medium heat for 10 minutes, stirring, until golden. Add the laksa paste and cook for 2 minutes.

2 Add the coconut milk, stock and baby corn and season with salt and pepper. Bring to the boil, reduce the heat and simmer for 5 minutes.

3 Add the salmon slices and spinach, stirring to immerse them in the liquid. Cook for 4 minutes until the fish is opaque all the way through.

4 Meanwhile, put the noodles in a large heatproof bowl, pour over boiling water to cover and soak for 30 seconds. Drain well, then stir them into the curry. Pour the curry into four serving bowls, garnish with the spring onions and coriander and serve with the lime wedges.

Preparation Time: 10 minutes

Cooking Time: about 20 minutes

Serves: 4

Calories Per Serving: 570

Try Something Different

Use haddock, coley or whiting instead of the cod.
Stir 1 tbsp capers in with the dill and wine.

Roasted Cod with Fennel

50g (2oz) butter

1 tbsp olive oil

2 red onions, finely sliced

2 small or 1 large fennel bulb, trimmed and finely sliced

2 tbsp chopped dill, plus extra to garnish

150ml (¼ pint) dry white wine

4 x 150g (5oz) pieces cod

salt and ground black pepper

new potatoes and green beans to serve

1 Preheat the oven to 200°C (180°C fan oven) mark 6. Heat the butter and olive oil in a flameproof casserole dish over a medium heat. When sizzling, add the onions and fennel, then cover and cook, stirring occasionally, for 7 minutes or until soft and translucent.

2 Add the dill and white wine and bring quickly to the boil. Put the fish on top of the fennel mixture and season with salt and pepper. Put the casserole dish in the oven and cook for 10 minutes, basting the fish occasionally with the juices.

3 Sprinkle with plenty of extra dill and serve immediately with new potatoes and green beans.

Preparation Time: 3 minutes

Cooking Time: 20 minutes

Serves: 4

Calories Per Serving: 306

Try Something Different

Use another fish instead of salmon; try trout or plump mackerel fillets.

3 tbsp freshly chopped coriander

1 garlic clove, crushed

2.5cm (1in) piece fresh root ginger, peeled and grated

½ tsp each ground cumin and coriander

¼ tsp cayenne pepper

150g (5oz) natural yogurt

4 x 125g (4oz) salmon fillets

salt

lime wedges and herb salad to serve

Salmon with a Spicy Yogurt Crust

1 Preheat the grill. Mix together the chopped coriander, garlic, ginger, cumin, ground coriander, cayenne, yogurt and a pinch of salt. Add the salmon and turn to coat.

2 Grill the fish for 7–10 minutes or until cooked through. Serve with lime wedges to squeeze over the fish and a herb salad.

Preparation Time: 10 minutes

Cooking Time: 10 minutes

Serves: 4

Calories Per Serving: 250

Try Something Different

Instead of mussels you could use 500g (1lb 2oz) large raw peeled prawns; simmer for 5 minutes until the prawns are pink and cooked through.

Thai Coconut Mussels

1 tbsp vegetable oil

2 shallots, finely chopped

2–3 tbsp Thai green curry paste

400ml can coconut milk

2kg (4½lb) mussels, scrubbed and beards removed

a small handful of fresh coriander, chopped, plus extra sprigs to garnish

1 Heat the vegetable oil in a large, deep pan. Add the shallots and curry paste and fry gently for 5 minutes, stirring regularly, until the shallots are starting to soften. Stir in the coconut milk, cover with a tight-fitting lid and bring to the boil.

2 Add the mussels to the pan, cover, shake the pan well and cook over a medium heat for 4–5 minutes. Give the pan another good shake. Check the mussels and discard any that are still closed. Stir in the chopped coriander and serve immediately, garnished with coriander sprigs.

Preparation Time: 15 minutes

Cooking Time: about 12 minutes

Serves: 4

Calories Per Serving: 210

Cook's Tips

If you can't find satay and sweet chilli pesto, substitute 2 tbsp peanut butter and 1 tbsp sweet chilli sauce.

Chilli soy sauce can be replaced with 2 tbsp light soy sauce and ½ red chilli, finely chopped (see page 17).

Quick Pad Thai

250g (9oz) wide ribbon rice noodles

3 tbsp satay and sweet chilli pesto (see Cook's Tip)

125g (4oz) mangetouts, thinly sliced

125g (4oz) sugarsnap peas, thinly sliced

3 eggs, beaten

3 tbsp chilli soy sauce, plus extra to serve (see Cook's Tip)

250g (9oz) cooked peeled tiger prawns

25g (1oz) dry-roasted peanuts, roughly crushed

lime wedges to serve (optional)

1 Put the noodles in a heatproof bowl, cover with boiling water and soak for 4 minutes until softened. Drain, rinse under cold water and set aside.

2 Heat a wok or large frying pan until hot, add the chilli pesto and stir-fry for 1 minute. Add the mangetouts and sugarsnap peas and cook for a further 2 minutes. Tip into a bowl. Put the pan back on the heat, add the eggs and cook, stirring, for 1 minute.

3 Add the soy sauce, prawns and noodles to the pan. Toss well and cook for 3 minutes until piping hot. Return the vegetables to the pan, cook for a further 1 minute until heated through, then sprinkle with the peanuts. Serve with extra soy sauce and lime wedges to squeeze over, if you like.

Preparation Time: 12 minutes, plus 4 minutes soaking

Cooking Time: 8 minutes

Serves: 4

Calories Per Serving: 451

2 large leeks, cut into chunks

2 large courgettes, sliced

2 fennel bulbs, cut into chunks

125ml (4fl oz) hot vegetable stock

zest of ½ lemon

4 salmon fillets, 100g (3½oz) each

15g (½oz) pinenuts, toasted

salt and ground black pepper

Salmon with Roasted Vegetables

1 Preheat the oven to 200°C (180°C fan oven) mark 6. Put the leeks into a roasting tin. Add the courgettes and fennel. Pour over the stock, season well with salt and pepper and roast for 30 minutes or until tender.

2 Meanwhile, sprinkle the lemon zest over the salmon and season. Put on a baking sheet lined with greaseproof paper and cook in the oven with the vegetables for the last 20 minutes of the cooking time.

3 Scatter the pinenuts over the roasted vegetables and mix together well. Divide the vegetables among four plates and top each with a piece of salmon.

Preparation Time: 10 minutes

Cooking Time: 30 minutes

Serves: 4

Calories Per Serving: 258

Cook's tip

Basmati rice should be washed before cooking to remove excess starch and to give really light, fluffy results.

250g (9oz) basmati rice

8 x 125g (4oz) tuna steaks

5cm (2in) piece fresh root ginger, peeled and grated

1 tbsp olive oil

100ml (3½fl oz) orange juice

300g (11oz) pak choi, roughly chopped

a small handful of freshly chopped coriander

ground black pepper

lime wedges to garnish

Tuna with Coriander Rice

1 Cook the rice according to the packet instructions. Meanwhile, put the tuna steaks in a shallow dish. Add the ginger, olive oil and orange juice, and season well with pepper. Turn the tuna over to coat.

2 Heat a non-stick frying pan until really hot. Add 4 tuna steaks and half the marinade. Cook for 1–2 minutes on each side until just cooked. Repeat with the remaining tuna and marinade. Remove the fish from the pan and keep warm.

3 Add the pak choi to the frying pan and cook for 1–2 minutes until wilted. When the rice is cooked, drain and stir the coriander through. Serve the tuna with the pak choi, rice and pan juices, and garnish with lime wedges.

Preparation Time: 5 minutes

Cooking Time: 10 minutes

Serves: 4

Calories Per Serving: 451

200g (7oz) fresh crabmeat

2 spring onions, finely chopped

2 red chillies, seeded and finely chopped (see page 17)

finely grated zest of 1 lime

4 tbsp freshly chopped coriander

about 40g (1½oz) stoneground wholemeal breadcrumbs

1 tbsp groundnut oil

1 tbsp plain flour

thinly sliced red chilli to garnish

1 lime, cut into wedges, and salad leaves to serve

Quick Crab Cakes

1 Put the crabmeat in a bowl, then mix with the spring onions, chillies, lime zest and coriander. Add enough breadcrumbs to hold the mixture together, then form into four small patties.

2 Heat ½ tbsp groundnut oil in a pan. Dredge the patties with flour and fry on one side for 3 minutes. Add the rest of the oil, turn the patties over and fry for a further 2–3 minutes. Garnish the crab cakes with thinly sliced red chilli and serve with lime wedges to squeeze over them, and salad leaves.

Preparation Time: 15 minutes

Cooking Time: 6 minutes

Serves: 4

Calories Per Serving: 124

Try Something Different

Try baby leaf spinach instead of watercress.
Use wholegrain mustard instead of horseradish.

Smoked Mackerel with Potato and Horseradish Salad

350g (12oz) new potatoes, scrubbed

2 tbsp horseradish sauce

2 tbsp crème fraîche

1 tbsp lemon juice

4 tbsp olive oil

2 crisp apples

2 smoked mackerel fillets

100g (3½oz) watercress

ground black pepper

1 Cook the potatoes in a pan of lightly salted boiling water for 15–20 minutes until tender. Drain and set aside.

2 In a bowl, mix together the horseradish sauce, crème fraîche, lemon juice and olive oil, then season with pepper.

3 Core and roughly chop the apples and chop the warm potatoes. Put both in a large bowl and toss in the dressing. Skin and flake the mackerel and add to the bowl with the watercress. Toss together and serve.

Preparation Time: 15 minutes

Cooking Time: 20 minutes

Serves: 4

Calories Per Serving: 320

Cook's Tip

To devein prawns, make a shallow cut along the back of the prawn and remove the black thread with the tip of your knife.

225g (8oz) peeled raw king prawns, deveined (see Cook's Tip)

550g (1¼lb) monkfish fillet, cut into 2.5cm (1in) cubes

juice of ½ lime

1 garlic clove, crushed

2 tbsp chilli oil

2 tbsp teriyaki sauce

2 limes and 1 lemon, each cut into 8 wedges

finely chopped and seeded green chilli (see page 17), spring onion curls (see page 99) and flat-leafed parsley to garnish

rice to serve

Seafood and Lime Kebabs

1 Put the prawns and monkfish in a bowl. Combine the lime juice, garlic, chilli oil and teriyaki sauce and pour over the top. Stir well to coat and leave in a cool place for up to 1 hour. Meanwhile, if using wooden skewers, soak eight in water for 30 minutes.

2 Remove the seafood from the marinade and thread on to the skewers interspersed with lime and lemon wedges.

3 Heat a griddle or grill. Grill the kebabs for 3 minutes, turning once during cooking and brushing with the marinade. Garnish with green chilli, spring onion curls and parsley, and serve with rice.

Preparation Time: 20 minutes, plus 1 hour marinating

Cooking Time: 3 minutes

Serves: 4

Calories Per Serving: 184

Cook's Tip

There's no need to turn the salmon over halfway through – just remember to keep a close eye on it and lower the heat if necessary, so that the honey in the sauce doesn't burn.

4 tbsp Dijon mustard-flavoured mayonnaise

4 tbsp finely chopped fresh dill

4 tbsp clear honey

1 tbsp lemon juice

4 thick skinless salmon fillets, about 150g (5oz) each

tomato salad to serve

Dill Salmon

1 Preheat the grill to high. Put the mayonnaise into a bowl with the dill, honey and lemon juice. Mix together.

2 Put the salmon fillets on to a baking sheet and spread the mayonnaise mixture over the top. Grill for 5–7 minutes, depending on the thickness, until just cooked. Serve with tomato salad.

Preparation Time: 2 minutes

Cooking Time: 5–7 minutes

Serves: 4

Calories Per Serving: 421

Try Something Different

Replace the cod with any firm-fleshed fish: try salmon, coley (saithe), pollack or whiting.

4 thick cod fillets, 175g (6oz) each

grated zest of 1 lime

1 tbsp chilli oil

1 tbsp sesame oil

1 red chilli, seeded and chopped (see page 17)

2 garlic cloves, chopped

8 spring onions, trimmed and sliced

125g (4oz) shiitake mushrooms, sliced

225g (8oz) carrots, cut into strips

300g (11oz) pak choi, chopped

2 tbsp soy sauce

salt and ground black pepper

lime wedges to serve

Cod with Oriental Vegetables

1 Put the cod in a shallow, non-metallic dish. Mix the lime zest with the chilli oil and rub over the fillets. Cover and leave in a cool place for 30 minutes.

2 Heat the sesame oil in a large frying pan, add the chilli, garlic, spring onions, mushrooms and carrots and stir-fry for 2–3 minutes until the vegetables begin to soften. Add the pak choi and stir-fry for 1–2 minutes. Add the soy sauce and cook for a further minute. Season with salt and pepper.

3 Meanwhile, grill the cod fillets under a medium-hot grill for 2–3 minutes on each side until the flesh has turned opaque and is firm to the touch.

4 Pile the stir-fried vegetables on top of the cod and serve with lime wedges.

Preparation Time: 10 minutes, plus 30 minutes marinating

Cooking Time: about 6 minutes

Serves: 4

Calories Per Serving: 284

Try Something Different

Replace the trout with 225g (8oz) cooked salmon, haddock or smoked haddock. Skin, flake and add at stage 2.

Unless you are on a wheat-free diet, you can replace the gluten-free flour with plain flour.

Trout and Dill Fishcakes

4 medium potatoes, peeled and chopped

2 trout fillets

3 spring onions, finely chopped

2 dill sprigs, finely chopped

zest of 1 lemon

1 tbsp olive oil

a little plain gluten-free flour

salt

watercress to serve

1 Cook the potatoes in a pan of lightly salted boiling water for 6–8 minutes until tender. Drain, return to the pan and mash.

2 Preheat the grill to high. Grill the trout fillets for 8–10 minutes until cooked through and firm to the touch. Skin the fish, flake into pieces, removing any bones, then put into the pan with the mashed potato.

3 Add the spring onions, dill and lemon zest to the pan with the olive oil, season with salt and mix together well.

4 Shape the mixture into eight small patties. Dust with flour and put on a non-stick baking sheet, then grill for 3 minutes on each side. Serve the fishcakes hot, with watercress.

Preparation Time: 15 minutes

Cooking Time: 25 minutes

Serves: 4

Calories Per Serving: 196

Tuna Salad

400g can mixed beans, drained and rinsed

125g (4oz) flaked tuna

½ cucumber, chopped

1 red onion, finely sliced

2 ripe tomatoes, chopped

2 celery sticks, chopped

handful of baby leaf spinach

1 tbsp olive oil

2 tsp red wine vinegar

salt and ground black pepper

1 Put the beans into a bowl and add the tuna, cucumber, red onion, tomatoes, celery and spinach.

2 Mix together the olive oil and wine vinegar, season with salt and pepper, then toss through the bean mix and serve.

Preparation Time: 10 minutes

Serves: 2

Calories Per Serving: 313

Cook's Tip

To make spring onion curls, trim spring onions into 7.5cm (3in) lengths, shred finely, then place in a bowl of water with ice cubes for 30 minutes.

8–12 large Chinese leaves or lettuce leaves

4 salmon steaks, about 150g (5oz) each

½ tsp sesame oil

2 tbsp dry sherry

2 tbsp light soy sauce, plus extra to serve

4 spring onions, shredded, plus extra spring onion curls to garnish (see Cook's Tip)

3 tsp sesame seeds, lightly toasted in a dry wok or heavy-based pan

ground white pepper

Steamed Sesame Salmon

1 Steam the Chinese leaves or lettuce leaves for 1–2 minutes until soft and pliable. Discard about 2.5cm (1in) of the firm stalk end from each leaf to neaten. Place 2–3 leaves together, slightly overlapping, for each parcel. Put a salmon steak on top of each.

2 Mix the sesame oil with the sherry and soy sauce and drizzle the mixture over the salmon. Sprinkle with the shredded spring onions, 2 tsp sesame seeds and pepper to taste.

3 Fold the leaves over the salmon to form neat parcels. Steam for 5–7 minutes or until the fish is cooked and flakes easily.

4 Serve the salmon parcels with the juices spooned over. Sprinkle with the remaining sesame seeds and a little extra soy sauce and garnish with spring onion curls.

Preparation Time: 20 minutes

Cooking Time: 15–18 minutes

Serves: 4

Calories Per Serving: 312

Cook's Tips

Nasi goreng is a spicy Indonesian dish traditionally eaten for breakfast. Nasi goreng paste can be bought at large supermarkets and Asian food shops.

If you can't find microwave rice, use 200g (7oz) long-grain rice, cooked according to the packet instructions – but do not overcook. Rinse in cold water and drain well before you begin the recipe.

Special Prawn Fried Rice

1 tbsp sesame oil

6 tbsp nasi goreng paste (see Cook's Tips)

200g (7oz) green cabbage, shredded

250g (9oz) cooked peeled large prawns

2 x 250g packs of microwave rice (see Cook's Tips)

2 tbsp light soy sauce

1 tbsp sunflower oil

2 eggs, beaten

2 spring onions, thinly sliced

1 lime, cut into wedges, to serve

1 Heat the sesame oil in a wok and fry the nasi goreng paste for 1–2 minutes. Add the cabbage and stir-fry for 2–3 minutes. Add the prawns and stir briefly, then add the rice and soy sauce and cook for a further 5 minutes, stirring occasionally.

2 To make the omelette, heat the sunflower oil in a non-stick frying pan (about 25.5cm/10in in diameter) and add the eggs. Swirl around to cover the base of the pan in a thin layer and cook for 2–3 minutes until set.

3 Roll up the omelette and cut it into strips. Serve the rice scattered with the omelette and spring onions, and pass around the lime wedges to squeeze over.

Preparation Time: 5 minutes

Cooking Time: 10–13 minutes

Serves: 4

Calories Per Serving: 412 calories

Scallops with Ginger

2 tbsp vegetable oil

500g (1lb 2oz) shelled large scallops, cut into 5mm (¼in) slices

4 celery sticks, sliced diagonally

1 bunch spring onions, sliced diagonally

25g (1oz) piece fresh root ginger, peeled and sliced

2 large garlic cloves, sliced

¼ tsp chilli powder

2 tbsp lemon juice

2 tbsp light soy sauce

3 tbsp freshly chopped coriander

salt and ground black pepper

1 Heat the vegetable oil in a wok or large frying pan. Add the scallops, celery, spring onions, ginger, garlic and chilli powder and stir-fry over a high heat for 2 minutes or until the vegetables are just tender.

2 Pour in the lemon juice and soy sauce, allow to bubble up, then stir in about 2 tbsp chopped coriander and season with salt and pepper. Serve immediately, sprinkled with the remaining coriander.

Preparation Time: 15 minutes

Cooking Time: 3 minutes

Serves: 4

Calories Per Serving: 197

Try Something Different

Instead of prawns, try chicken cut into strips; stir-fry for 5 minutes in step 1.

Five-minute Stir-fry

1 tbsp sesame oil

175g (6oz) raw peeled tiger prawns, deveined

50ml (2fl oz) ready-made sweet chilli and ginger sauce

225g (8oz) ready-prepared mixed stir-fry vegetables, such as sliced courgettes, broccoli and green beans

1 Heat the sesame oil in a large wok or frying pan, add the prawns and sweet chilli and ginger sauce and stir-fry for 2 minutes.

2 Add the mixed vegetables and stir-fry for a further 2–3 minutes until the prawns are cooked and the vegetables are heated through. Serve immediately.

Preparation Time: 2 minutes

Cooking Time: 5 minutes

Serves: 2

Calories Per Serving: 170

Cook's Tips

Soba noodles are made from buckwheat and are gluten-free. If you have a wheat allergy or gluten intolerance, look for 100% soba on the pack.
Furikake seasoning is a Japanese condiment consisting of sesame seeds and chopped seaweed and can be found in major supermarkets and Asian food shops.

550g (1¼lb) salmon fillet, cut into 1cm (½in) slices

3 tbsp teriyaki sauce

3 tbsp tamari or light soy sauce

2 tbsp vegetable oil

1 tbsp sesame oil

1 tbsp chopped fresh chives

2 tsp grated fresh root ginger

2 garlic cloves, crushed

350g (12oz) soba noodles (see Cook's Tips)

350g (12oz) baby leaf spinach

furikake seasoning (see Cook's Tips)

Teriyaki Salmon with Spinach

1 Gently mix the salmon slices with the teriyaki sauce, then cover, chill and leave to marinate for 1 hour.

2 Mix together the tamari or soy sauce, 1 tbsp vegetable oil, the sesame oil, chives, ginger and garlic. Set aside.

3 Cook the noodles according to the packet instructions. Drain and put to one side.

4 Heat the remaining vegetable oil in a wok or large frying pan. Remove the salmon from the marinade and add it to the pan. Cook over a high heat until it turns opaque – about 30 seconds. Remove from the pan and put to one side.

5 Add the drained noodles to the pan and stir until warmed through. Stir in the spinach and cook for 1–2 minutes until wilted. Add the soy sauce mixture and stir to combine.

6 Divide the noodles among four deep bowls, then top with the salmon. Sprinkle with furikake seasoning and serve.

Preparation Time: 10 minutes, plus 1 hour marinating

Cooking Time: 6 minutes

Serves: 4

Calories Per Serving: 672

Try Something Different

Use cleaned squid or mussels instead of scallops and prawns.

Thai Green Shellfish Curry

1 tbsp vegetable oil

1 lemongrass stalk, chopped

2 small red chillies, chopped (see page 17)

a handful of coriander leaves, chopped, plus extra to serve

2 kaffir lime leaves, chopped

1–2 tbsp Thai green curry paste

400ml can coconut milk

450ml (¾ pint) vegetable stock

375g (13oz) queen scallops with corals

250g (9oz) raw tiger prawns, peeled and deveined, with tails intact

salt and ground black pepper

jasmine rice to serve

1 Heat the vegetable oil in a wok or large frying pan. Add the lemongrass, chillies, coriander and lime leaves and stir-fry for 30 seconds. Add the curry paste and fry for 1 minute.

2 Add the coconut milk and stock and bring to the boil. Simmer for 5–10 minutes until slightly reduced. Season well with salt and pepper.

3 Add the scallops and tiger prawns, bring to the boil and simmer gently for 2–3 minutes until cooked. Divide the jasmine rice among six serving bowls and spoon the curry over the top. Sprinkle with coriander and serve immediately, with rice.

Preparation Time: 10 minutes

Cooking Time: 10–15 minutes

Serves: 6

Calories Per Serving: 156

Health Tip

Oily fish such as sardines are one of the best sources of omega-3 oils, essential for good health. Eat them at least once a week. Fresh Cornish sardines, when they are available, are a treat and are cheap. Look out for them at your fishmongers or on the fresh fish counter at the supermarket.

Grilled Sardines with Harissa

1 garlic clove, crushed

2 tbsp olive oil

1–2 tsp harissa

4 whole sardines

salt and ground black pepper

tomato salad, watercress and lime wedges to serve

1 Preheat the grill to high. Put the garlic in a bowl. Add the olive oil and harissa, season to taste with salt and pepper, and mix together.

2 Slash the sardines a couple of times on each side, then brush the harissa and oil mixture all over. Grill for 5–10 minutes on each side until cooked through.

3 Serve with tomato salad, watercress and lime wedges to squeeze over the sardines.

Preparation Time: 10 minutes

Cooking Time: 10–20 minutes

Serves: 2

Calories Per Serving: 292

Try Something Different

Instead of squid, try 400g (14oz) rump steak, cut into thin strips.

Squid and Vegetables in Black Bean Sauce

2 tbsp black bean sauce

1 tbsp Thai fish sauce

2–3 tsp clear honey

75ml (2½fl oz) fish or vegetable stock

1 tbsp tamarind juice

2 tsp cornflour

450g (1lb) cleaned squid

50g (2oz) each broccoli, carrots and mangetouts

2 tbsp sesame seeds

2 tbsp sunflower oil

1 tbsp sesame oil

2 garlic cloves

2 dried red chillies

75g (3oz) cauliflower, cut into small florets

1 small green or red pepper, seeded and thinly sliced

50g (2oz) Chinese cabbage or pak choi, shredded

25g (1oz) bean sprouts

2 tbsp fresh coriander, roughly torn

Preparation Time: 35 minutes

Cooking Time: 10–15 minutes

Serves: 4

Calories Per Serving: 274

1 First, prepare the sauce. In a small bowl, mix together the black bean sauce, fish sauce, honey and stock. Add the tamarind juice and cornflour and whisk until smooth. Set aside.

2 Wash and dry the squid, and halve the tentacles if large. Open out the body pouches, score diagonally, then cut into large squares; set aside. Cut the broccoli into florets and thinly slice the carrots.

3 Toast the sesame seeds in a dry wok or large frying pan over a medium heat, stirring until they turn golden. Tip on to a plate.

4 Heat the sunflower and sesame oils in the same pan. Add the garlic and chillies and fry gently for 5 minutes. Remove the garlic and chillies with a slotted spoon and discard.

5 Add all the vegetables to the pan and stir-fry for 3 minutes. Add the squid, increase the heat and stir-fry for a further 2 minutes until the squid curls up and turns opaque. Add the sauce and allow to simmer for 1 minute.

6 Scatter over the sesame seeds and coriander and serve immediately.

2 tbsp teriyaki marinade

juice of ½ lime

1 tbsp sweet chilli sauce

1 tbsp honey

4 tuna steaks, 125g (4oz) each

750ml (1¼ pints) hot vegetable stock

2 tbsp dry sherry

200g (7oz) medium egg noodles

200g (7oz) pak choi, roughly chopped

2 carrots, cut into matchsticks

250g (9oz) button mushrooms, sliced

freshly chopped coriander (optional)

Teriyaki Tuna with Noodle Broth

1 Mix together the teriyaki marinade, lime juice, chilli sauce and honey in a large, shallow dish. Add the tuna and toss to coat.

2 Put the stock and sherry into a pan and bring to the boil. Add the noodles and cook for 4–5 minutes, then stir in the pak choi, carrots and mushrooms. Simmer for 1 minute.

3 Meanwhile, heat a frying pan until hot. Fry the tuna in the marinade for 2 minutes on each side until just cooked and still slightly pink inside. Cut into thick slices.

4 When the noodles are cooked, divide among four wide bowls, spoon the broth over them, then top each with the tuna and a sprinkling of coriander, if you like.

Preparation Time: 10 minutes

Cooking Time: 10 minutes

Serves: 4

Calories Per Serving: 411

Desserts

Get Ahead

Make up to a day beforehand. Put into an airtight container and chill.
To use Take out of the refrigerator and allow to reach room temperature (around 30 minutes) before serving.

Summer Fruit Compote

12 fresh, ripe apricots, halved and stoned

125g (4oz) fresh blueberries

50g (2oz) vanilla sugar

juice of 1 orange

200g (7oz) strawberries, hulled and halved

Greek yogurt to serve

1 Preheat the oven to 180°C (160°C fan oven) mark 4. Put the apricots, blueberries, vanilla sugar and orange juice into a large, shallow baking dish and bake, uncovered, for about 20 minutes or until just tender.

2 Gently stir in the strawberries. Taste the cooking juices – you may want to add a little extra sugar – then leave to cool. Cover and chill. Serve with a spoonful of Greek yogurt.

Preparation Time: 10 minutes

Cooking Time: 20 minutes, plus cooling and chilling

Serves: 4

Calories Per Serving: 122

Try Something Different

This is just as good with mangoes and orange syrup; use 1 orange instead of 2 limes.

Papaya with Lime Syrup

75g (3oz) golden caster sugar

zest and juice of 2 limes

2 papayas, peeled, halved and seeds removed

1 Put the caster sugar in a small pan with 100ml (3½fl oz) water and the lime zest and juice. Heat gently to dissolve the sugar, then bring to the boil and bubble rapidly for 5 minutes or until the mixture is reduced and syrupy.

2 Cut the papayas into slices and arrange on a large serving plate. Drizzle over the lime syrup and serve.

Preparation Time: 10 minutes

Cooking Time: 10 minutes

Serves: 4

Calories Per Serving: 200

Sweet Kebabs

chocolate brownie, about 10 x 5cm (4 x 2in), cut into eight chunks

8 large strawberries

whipped cream to serve

1 Spear alternate chunks of chocolate brownie and strawberries on to skewers; barbecue or grill for 3 minutes, turning occasionally. Serve with whipped cream.

Preparation Time: 5 minutes

Cooking Time: 3 minutes

Serves: 4

Calories Per Serving: 521

Try Something Different

Use blackberries instead of rhubarb: you will need 400g (14oz), and a squeeze of lemon juice instead of the orange juice. Blend in a food processor after stirring in the redcurrant jelly.
Use Greek yogurt if you can't find the fat-free Greek-style variety.

Rhubarb Fool

450g (1lb) rhubarb, thickly chopped

50ml (2fl oz) orange juice

1 cinnamon stick

25g (1oz) golden caster sugar

1 tbsp redcurrant jelly

150g (5oz) fat-free Greek-style yogurt

2 tbsp soft brown sugar

1 Put the rhubarb, orange juice, cinnamon stick and caster sugar into a pan. Cover and cook gently for 10 minutes or until tender.

2 Remove the lid and cook for 5 minutes until the liquid has evaporated. Discard the cinnamon stick. Stir in the redcurrant jelly then leave to cool.

3 Roughly fold in the yogurt, then spoon the mixture into six glasses and sprinkle with the soft brown sugar. Chill for 2 hours before serving.

Preparation Time: 5 minutes, plus chilling

Cooking Time: 10 minutes

Serves: 6

Calories Per Serving: 107

Cook's tip

Look for firm, thin-skinned oranges that are heavy for their size – they will be more juicy.

Oranges with Caramel Sauce

6 oranges

25g (1oz) butter

2 tbsp golden caster sugar

2 tbsp Grand Marnier

2 tbsp orange marmalade

zest and juice of 1 large orange

crème fraîche to serve

1 Preheat the oven to 200°C (180°C fan oven) mark 6. Cut away the peel and pith from the oranges, then put them into a roasting tin just large enough to hold them.

2 Melt the butter in a pan and add the caster sugar, Grand Marnier, marmalade, orange zest and juice, then heat gently to dissolve the sugar. Pour over the oranges. Bake for 30–40 minutes. Serve with crème fraîche.

Preparation Time: 15 minutes

Cooking Time: 40 minutes

Serves: 6

Calories Per Serving: 139

Strawberry and Black Pepper Granita

400g (14oz) hulled strawberries

75g (3oz) golden caster sugar

juice of ½ lemon

ground black pepper

1 Whiz the strawberries to a purée in a food processor or blender. Add the caster sugar, lemon juice and a good grinding of black pepper. Stir in 450ml (¾ pint) water. Pulse to mix, then pour into a freezerproof container.

2 Freeze for 2 hours. Use a fork to stir in the frozen edges then freeze again for 1 hour. Fork through, then freeze for a further 1 hour or overnight. Use a fork to break up the granita, then serve in tall glasses.

Preparation Time: 10 minutes, plus freezing

Serves: 6

Calories Per Serving: 67

Try Something Different

Use a cinnamon stick instead of the star anise.

Nectarines in Spiced Honey and Lemon

4 tbsp clear honey

2 star anise

1 tbsp freshly squeezed lemon juice

150ml (¼ pint) boiling water

4 ripe nectarines or peaches, halved and stoned

vanilla ice cream to serve (optional)

1 Put the honey, star anise and lemon juice in a heatproof bowl. Stir in the boiling water and leave until just warm.

2 Add the nectarines or peaches to the bowl and leave to cool. Transfer to a glass serving dish. Serve with a scoop of vanilla ice cream, if you like.

Preparation Time: 10 minutes, plus cooling

Serves: 4

Calories Per Serving: 95

Chocolate Cinnamon Sorbet

200g (7oz) golden granulated sugar

50g (2oz) unsweetened cocoa powder

1 tsp instant espresso coffee powder

1 cinnamon stick

8 tsp crème de cacao (chocolate liqueur) to serve (optional)

1 Put the granulated sugar, cocoa powder, coffee and cinnamon stick into a large pan with 600ml (1 pint) water. Bring to the boil, stirring until the sugar has completely dissolved. Boil for 5 minutes, then remove from the heat. Leave to cool. Remove the cinnamon stick, then chill.

2 If you have an ice-cream maker, put the mixture into it and churn for about 30 minutes until firm. Otherwise, pour into a freezerproof container and put in the coldest part of the freezer until firmly frozen, then transfer the frozen mixture to a blender or food processor and blend until smooth. Quickly put the mixture back in the container and return it to the freezer for at least 1 hour.

3 To serve, scoop the sorbet into individual cups and, if you like, drizzle 1 tsp chocolate liqueur over each portion. Serve immediately.

Preparation Time: 5 minutes, plus chilling and freezing

Cooking Time: 15 minutes

Serves: 8

Calories Per Serving: 118

Try Something Different

Orange sorbet: replace two of the lemons with oranges.
Lime sorbet: replace two of the lemons with four limes.

Lemon Sorbet

3 juicy unwaxed lemons

125g (4oz) golden caster sugar

1 large egg white

1 Finely pare the lemon zest, using a zester, then squeeze the juice. Put the zest into a pan with the caster sugar and 350ml (12fl oz) water and heat gently until the sugar has dissolved. Increase the heat and boil for 10 minutes. Leave to cool.

2 Stir the lemon juice into the cooled sugar syrup. Cover and chill in the fridge for 30 minutes.

3 Strain the syrup through a fine sieve into a bowl. In another bowl, beat the egg white until just frothy, then whisk into the lemon mixture.

4 For best results, freeze in an ice-cream maker. Otherwise, pour into a shallow freezerproof container and freeze until almost frozen; mash well with a fork and freeze until solid. Transfer the sorbet to the fridge 30 minutes before serving to soften slightly.

Preparation Time: 10 minutes, plus chilling and freezing

Serves: 4

Calories Per Serving: 130

Try Something Different

If watermelon is not in season use another variety of melon, such as Charentais, Canteloupe or Galia. If you are using one of the sweeter varieties, reduce the honey to about 1 tbsp.

2 tbsp pinenuts

½ watermelon

50g (2oz) feta cheese

2 tbsp clear honey

a handful of roughly chopped mint

Watermelon with Feta and Honey

1 Put the pinenuts in a small pan and toast over a medium-high heat, tossing occasionally, until golden-brown all over, about 2–3 minutes. Cool.

2 Cut the rind off the watermelon, and cut into chunks. Arrange on a serving plate. Crumble the feta cheese over the melon and drizzle the honey over.

3 Scatter with the pinenuts and mint and serve.

Preparation Time: 10 minutes

Cooking Time: 3 minutes

Serves: 4

Calories Per Serving: 182

Try Something Different

Use nectarines instead of peaches, and raspberries or blueberries instead of strawberries.

Poached Peaches and Strawberries

4 ripe peaches, halved, stoned and quartered

250ml (9fl oz) orange juice

½ tbsp golden caster sugar

a small pinch of ground cinnamon

225g (8oz) halved strawberries

1 Put the peaches in a pan with the orange juice, caster sugar and cinnamon. Simmer gently for 5 minutes. Remove the peaches with a slotted spoon and put in a bowl.

2 Let the juice bubble until reduced by half. Pour over the peaches, then cool, cover and chill. Remove from the refrigerator about 2 hours before serving and stir in the halved strawberries.

Preparation Time: 10 minutes, plus chilling

Cooking Time: 10 minutes, plus cooling and chilling

Serves: 4

Calories Per Serving: 82

Apple and Raspberry Mousse

900g (2lb) cooking apples, peeled, cored and sliced

4 tbsp orange juice

grated zest of 1 lemon

225g (8oz) raspberries

6 tbsp golden caster sugar

1 large egg white

mint sprigs to decorate

1 Put the apples and orange juice into a pan and cook over a low heat, uncovered, for 10 minutes until soft. Add the lemon zest, then use a fork to mash to a purée. Cover and chill for at least 1 hour.

2 Gently heat the raspberries and 2 tbsp caster sugar in a pan until the juices start to run.

3 Whisk the egg white in a clean grease-free bowl until stiff, adding the remaining sugar gradually until the mixture forms stiff peaks. Fold into the apple purée.

4 Divide the raspberries and any juice among six serving glasses, spoon the apple mixture on top and decorate with mint sprigs. Serve immediately.

Preparation Time: 10 minutes, plus chilling

Cooking Time: 15 minutes

Serves: 6

Calories Per Serving: 127

Try Something Different

Use raspberries instead of strawberries, leaving them whole.
Try lightly toasted flaked almonds instead of the hazelnuts.

Strawberries with Chocolate Meringue

225g (8oz) strawberries, chopped

finely grated zest of ½ orange

125g (4oz) caster sugar, plus 1 tbsp extra

3 large egg whites

1 tbsp cocoa powder, sifted

15g (½oz) hazelnuts, toasted and chopped

1 Preheat the oven to 150°C (130°C fan oven) mark 2. Mix together the strawberries, orange zest and 1 tbsp caster sugar. Divide among six ramekins.

2 Put the egg whites into a clean grease-free bowl and whisk until soft peaks form. Add the remaining sugar and whisk until the whites are stiff and shiny. Fold in the cocoa.

3 Spoon the chocolate meringue over the fruit and sprinkle the hazelnuts on top.

4 Bake in the oven for 20–25 minutes until the meringue is crisp on the outside and soft in the middle. Serve immediately.

Preparation Time: 15 minutes

Cooking Time: 20–25 minutes

Serves: 6

Calories Per Serving: 132

Warm Plum Brioche Toasts

8 plums, halved and stoned

butter to grease

2 tbsp fruit liqueur, such as Kirsch

2 tbsp golden caster sugar

1 vanilla pod, split

grilled brioche and mascarpone to serve

1 Put the halved plums on a large piece of buttered foil. Sprinkle over the fruit liqueur and caster sugar and add the split vanilla pod. Scrunch the edges of the foil together to make a loose parcel.

2 Put the foil parcel on the barbecue and cook for 10 minutes. Serve hot, with lightly grilled brioche slices and mascarpone cheese.

Preparation Time: 10 minutes

Cooking Time: 10 minutes

Serves: 8

Calories Per Serving: 46

3 large fresh figs, quartered

1 large ripe mango, peeled, stoned and cubed

1 baby pineapple or 2 thick slices of pineapple, peeled, cored and cubed

1 tbsp dark runny honey

For the spiced pear dip

150g (5oz) ready-to-eat dried pears, soaked in hot water for about 30 minutes

juice of 1 orange

1 tsp finely chopped fresh root ginger

½ tsp vanilla extract

50g (2oz) very low-fat natural yogurt

½ tsp ground cinnamon, plus extra to dust

1 tsp dark runny honey

25g (1oz) hazelnuts, toasted and roughly chopped

Fruit Kebabs with Spiced Pear Dip

1 To make the dip, drain the pears and place in a food processor or blender with the orange juice, ginger, vanilla extract, yogurt, cinnamon and 50ml (2fl oz) water and process until smooth. Spoon the dip into a bowl. Drizzle with the honey, sprinkle with the toasted hazelnuts and dust with a little ground cinnamon. Cover and set aside in a cool place until ready to serve.

2 Preheat the grill to its highest setting. To make the kebabs, thread pieces of fruit on to six 20cm (8in) wooden skewers, using at least two pieces of each type of fruit per skewer. Place the skewers on a foil-covered tray and cover the ends of the skewers with strips of foil to prevent them burning. Drizzle with honey and grill for about 4 minutes on each side, close to the heat, until lightly charred. Serve warm or at room temperature with the dip.

Preparation Time: 5 minutes

Cooking Time: 20 minutes

Serves: 6

Calories Per Serving: 130

Try Something Different

Fresh apricots or greengages, halved and stoned, may be substituted for the cherries.

Clafoutis

1 Put the cherries in a bowl with the kirsch and 1 tbsp caster sugar. Mix together, cover and set aside for 1 hour.

2 Meanwhile, whisk the eggs with the remaining caster sugar and the flour. Bring the milk and cream to the boil and pour on to the egg mixture; whisk until combined. Add the vanilla extract and strain into a bowl, cover and set aside for 30 minutes.

3 Preheat the oven to 180°C (160°C fan oven) mark 4. Lightly butter a 1.7 litre (3 pint) shallow ovenproof dish and dust with caster sugar. Spoon the cherries into the dish, whisk the batter and pour it over them. Bake in the oven for 50–60 minutes or until golden and just set. Dust with icing sugar and serve warm with cream.

350g (12oz) stoned cherries

3 tbsp Kirsch

1 tbsp golden caster sugar

4 large eggs

100g (3½oz) caster sugar, plus 1 tbsp extra to dust

25g (1oz) flour

150ml (¼ pint) milk

150ml (¼ pint) single cream

1 tsp vanilla extract

icing sugar to dust

thick cream to serve

Preparation Time: 25 minutes, plus resting
Cooking Time: 1 hour
Serves: 6
Calories Per Serving: 235

Luxury Chocolate Orange Torte

75g (3oz) butter, diced, plus extra to grease

100g (3½oz) plain chocolate (at least 70% cocoa solids), broken into pieces

6 eggs

225g (8oz) golden caster sugar

150g (5oz) ground almonds, sifted

grated zest and juice of 1 orange

strawberries and raspberries to serve

1 Preheat the oven to 190°C (170°C fan oven) mark 5. Grease a 20cm (8in) springform cake tin and line with greaseproof paper.

2 Melt the butter and chocolate in a heatproof bowl set over a pan of gently simmering water. Remove the bowl from the pan and set aside to cool a little.

3 Put the eggs and caster sugar into a large bowl and mix with an electric whisk until the volume has tripled and the mixture is thick and foamy – it will take about 5–10 minutes. Add the ground almonds, orange zest and juice to the egg mixture, then gently fold together with a metal spoon.

4 Pour about two-thirds of the mixture into the prepared tin. Add the melted chocolate and butter to the remaining mixture and fold together. Add to the tin and swirl around just once or twice to create a marbled effect. Bake in the oven for 50 minutes–1 hour. Leave to cool in the tin, then carefully remove and slice. Serve with strawberries and raspberries.

Preparation Time: 30 minutes

Cooking Time: 55 minutes–1 hour 5 minutes

Serves: 12

Calories Per Serving: 231

First published in Great Britain in 2008
by Collins & Brown
10 Southcombe Street
London W14 0RA

An imprint of Anova Books
Company Ltd

Copyright © The National Magazine
Company Limited
and Collins & Brown 2008

The recipes in this volume have been
selected from Good Housekeeping's
Easy To Make series. For more titles in
this series see the back of this book.

The Good Housekeeping website is
www.goodhousekeeping.co.uk

10 9 8 7 6 5 4 3 2 1

ISSN 9771757665002

Reproduction by Dot Gradations Ltd
Printed and bound by Times Offset,
Malaysia

www.anovabooks.com